NOTES FROM A QUEER CRIPPLE

of related interest

Trans and Disabled
An Anthology of Identities and Experiences
Edited by Alex Iantaffi
ISBN 978 1 83997 080 1
eISBN 978 1 83997 081 8

Queer Sex
A Trans and Non-Binary Guide to Intimacy,
Pleasure and Relationships
Juno Roche
ISBN 978 1 78592 406 4
eISBN 978 1 78450 770 1

Queer Body Power
Finding Your Body Positivity
Essie Dennis
ISBN 978 1 78775 904 6
eISBN 978 1 78775 905 3

How to Do Life With a Chronic Illness
Reclaim Your Identity, Create Independence,
and Find Your Way Forward
Pippa Stacey
ISBN 978 1 80501 017 3
eISBN 978 1 80501 018 0

Notes from a **Queer Cripple**

How to Cultivate Queer Disabled Joy (and Be Hot While Doing It!)

Andrew Gurza

Jessica Kingsley Publishers
London and Philadelphia

First published in Great Britain in 2025 by Jessica Kingsley Publishers
Part of John Murray Press

1

Copyright © Andrew Gurza 2025

Content warning: This book contains sexual content,
and mention of ableism.

A CIP catalogue record for this title is available from the
British Library and the Library of Congress

ISBN 978 1 83997 818 0
eISBN 978 1 83997 819 7

Printed and bound in the United States
by Integrated Books International

Jessica Kingsley Publishers' policy is to use papers that are natural,
renewable and recyclable products and made from wood grown
in sustainable forests. The logging and manufacturing processes
are expected to conform to the environmental regulations
of the country of origin.

Jessica Kingsley
Carmelite House
50 Victoria Embankment
London EC4Y 0DZ

www.jkp.com

John Murray Press
Part of Hodder & Stoughton Limited
An Hachette UK Company

The authorised representative in the EEA is Hachette Ireland,
8 Castlecourt Centre, Dublin 15, D15 YF6A, Ireland (email: info@hbgi.ie)

Contents

CHAPTER 1

How Ableism Affects Queer Disabled People

f you read the chapter title and thought to yourself, "Wow, Andrew, that's an intense way to start a chapter off!", welcome! Hi! Hello! I'm so happy you are here! I wanted to cut right to the quick and make my first note, if you will, all about how ableism has an impact on queer disabled people because it is something that we simply don't explore enough. It is one part of the intersection of queerness and disability that far too often stays in the dark, and one that I want to give a big bright light to right away.

In order to really dive into how ableism feels, we have to get a few things out of the way. So, let me share with you the structure of this chapter. First, I want to make sure that we all have an understanding of key terminologies in this book: disability, ableism and internalized ableism, as I understand them. Within these definitions, we're going to get really personal. I'll share my personal stories navigating what it means to be disabled from my perspective, moments when I have dealt with ableism and how I feel about ableism in our world today, and lastly, how internalized ableism has impacted my sense of self as a disabled person.

From here, I'll be sharing stories about how ableism impacted my queerness as a disabled person, and highlighting how that made me feel. What impact did ableism have on my queer crippled identity, and most importantly, what did that feel like? My hope with this chapter is that queer disabled readers will feel not so alone, while non-disabled readers will be welcomed into a world that may seem unfamiliar at first, but by the end will positively change their worldview. So, come learn with me!

What is disability?

Defining disability is something that so many disabled people have trouble doing succinctly, simply because disability impacts each and every one of us living with it a little differently. For me, it means that I have been unable to do things like walking, dressing or changing since I was born; it means using a wheelchair as my mobility aid every day, all day. For me, my disabilities are both visible and invisible in nature; I live with cerebral palsy *and* anxiety, depression and irritable bowel syndrome, so I am a whole fun bag of conditions all rolled into a sexy, seated package.

All kidding aside, let me offer you my definition of disability. I would say that disability is something that we will all experience in our lifetime, and it will limit our ability to do things. It may mean that we need mobility aids, attendant care or other assistance throughout our lives, but it does not diminish our personhood.

What is ableism?

Ableism:

> Ableism is a set of beliefs or practices that devalue and discriminate against people with physical, intellectual, or psychiatric disabilities and often rests on the assumption that disabled people need to be "fixed" in one form or the other. Ableism is intertwined in our culture, due to many limiting beliefs about what disability does or does not mean, how able-bodied people learn to treat people with disabilities and how we are often not included at the table for key decisions.[1]

Now, this is ableism at its most basic. As a severely disabled queer person, I see ableism in our humor, in the way our queer community has been built to specifically cater to non-disabled community members, in the way the queer community can espouse unrealistic body ideals on one another, and so much more. Ableism is ever present in queer spaces, and I'll talk about that more as we go forward in this book.

What is internalized ableism?

Internalized ableism is when you take all of the messaging from the ableist system, and you begin to believe that about yourself. The effects of internalized ableism on the disabled person's

1   Smith, L. (2023). #Ableism—Center for Disability Rights. Cdrnys.org. https://cdrnys. org/blog/uncategorized/ableism.

self-esteem can be quite detrimental. As a queer cripple, I struggle in the aftermath of internalized ableism constantly: second-guessing my desirability and sexual worth, telling myself that my disability means I'm not good enough, or that no matter what I do I will always be a burden to the people around me. I consider my disability to be a big part of who I am, but if I am honest, so too is the internalized ableism that I carry with me on a daily basis, and it is a constant struggle to ward off the voices in my head that tell me these things.

How ableism impacted me

When I was a little boy in the playground, one day at recess I got into an argument with a little non-disabled girl. Who knows what our squabble was about; perhaps over a toy or something one of us had said (let me make very clear that despite my cute face, and wheelchair that was too big for my body at the time, I was no angel). I remember that as we began to fight with each other, the girl stopped and shouted, "Well, I hope your whole family ends up in a wheelchair!" As she said this, I remember stopping dead in my tracks and immediately starting to cry. Right at that moment, I realized that disability, particularly my experience of it as a kid in a wheelchair, was seen as a bad thing. It was seen as something to be looked down on.

My family was very good at simply folding my disability into our lives, and so while I knew I was disabled, I was shielded from the public scrutiny of it, until that moment. Moments like this one have shaped my perception of disability, and that's why I tell people that I am proudly disabled—because I don't want them to equate disability with a bad thing. Along with being proud of my disability status, this is also why in my definition of disability, I highlight that disability will be encountered by us all. I want people to understand that disability has no moral value, and when it happens, they won't want to be prejudged because of it.

When I was 25, I was looking to finish my master's thesis. I knew that I wanted to do something on disability and the law, but when I asked around for courses that examined this subject I was told that my university didn't have one. I remember inquiring why this was the case, and no one could answer me. I decided to create my own independent study unit to explore disability and its place in law. It was at this point, when I was building my outline for this, that I learned about ableism. I read stories from people who were denied access to buildings, classrooms, community groups, public transportation and so much more. I remember reading about the incredible Judy Heumann's 504 Sit-in[2] to push for disability rights and being absolutely transfixed at the lengths that she went to in order to combat ableism. I sat in my dorm room back in 2010, finally understanding that I had these feelings too. It finally clicked in me that I'd had these feelings since I was a child—like that day on the playground—but I'd never had the language for them.

Once I had the language of ableism, I began to see it everywhere I went: out on the street, in the jokes people made, the

---

2   On April 5, 1977, a group of people with disabilities staged a sit-in protest in San Francisco to demand greater accessibility and accommodations for people with disabilities. This historic protest became known as the "504 Sit-in." This protest progressed disability rights in America and helped pave the way for the Americans with Disabilities Act (ADA) to become law later on. https://disabilityrightsflorida.org/blog/entry/504-sit-in-history.

lack of accessibility at Pride events. It was staring me right in the face ALL. THE. TIME. Ableism was everywhere, and for a long time (and sometimes still), I was really angry about that. I was angry that I couldn't go out to the big queer parties, or hook up when and how I wanted to—and trust me, that anger is very, very real.

But now, I see ableism as a system of oppression that people need to be educated about. I love using my platforms to give people a lightbulb moment and to learn about ableism without anger or resentment from me. I love helping them to see that ableism doesn't make someone a bad person, it just means there are things that one might need to work on to get closer to being anti-ableist. Even though ableism impacts me every day, it also helps me change someone's mind about queer disabled people like me, and I am so thankful for that.

How ableism has directly impacted my queer crippled identity

I want to explain how ableism has had an impact on my queer disabled identity, and I want to share some stories to illustrate that with you. So, let's get comfy, cozy and crippled and crack into it.

My coming out (the first time)

In my journey of queerness, I have come out so many times; first as gay, then as queer, now as queer non-binary (the discovery won't ever truly stop). I have also come out time and time again as disabled in queer spaces, but for now, I want to share my first coming out story, and the role ableism played in it. I came out April 22, 1999, two weeks shy of my 16th birthday. At the time, the coming out narrative was still full of stories of queer people being kicked out of their homes, and we were certainly not in the progressive place we are in today. I had the added fear of being queer and disabled to add to my experience. I already felt like a burden just by being disabled, and now I was going to add being gay to my list of faults too.

For the longest time I swallowed down the feelings—I even had imaginary crushes on TV stars like Neve Campbell to "prove" I was straight. I remember going past my high school guidance counselor's office and seeing pamphlets that said "It's OK to Be Gay" but never "It's OK to Be Gay & Disabled." Finally, one night, after I'd spent about two weeks being a sullen teenager and blasting Alanis Morissette's "Jagged Little Pill" from the cassette player my stepdad set up in my room, the truth was out. We had just finished dinner, and as was our usual custom, my mom helped me finish my last bit of dinner and I chatted with her as she cleaned up the kitchen. On this night, I think she was tired of my teenaged woes and monosyllabic replies, and so she finally asked: "What's the matter? Are you gay?"

I was taken aback that she had got it right so quickly. I remember sitting in my wheelchair, staring at her as she stood over our bright red kitchen sink doing that night's dishes. I barely squeaked out a timid "Yeah." Then I remember that she said, "Oh." She stopped and looked right at me, and I burst into tears as all the fear I had spilled out. She hugged me tight and said she loved me. She sat with me as we ate my comfort food, yogurt and honey, and she asked if I thought Brad Pitt was hot.

Then, we rented *Priscilla, Queen of the Desert* to watch together and she told me that if I wanted to do drag I could.

While I was relieved by her acceptance of my identity, I think what I was most thankful for in that moment was her warning. She told me that gay men weren't going to know how to handle my disability. I can remember thinking in my teenage righteousness how wrong she was, but looking back on that moment she could not have been more right.

The drag show

In 2004, it was my freshman year in university. During Campus Pride Week that year, there was a drag show and one of my friends encouraged me to do it. She was really, really excited for me, because we didn't think that there had been a disabled person in the drag scene at my school before. Up to this point, I had never considered doing drag at all. If I'm honest, I was clinging to this idea of hyper-masculinity and internalized homophobia, which was also wrapped up in internalized ableism too—fun!

Despite my reservations, I understood the importance of having a wheelchair user like me at that drag competition, so I applied. A couple weeks later, I received an email from the 2SLGBTQ+ (two spirit, lesbian, gay, bisexual, transgender, queer and questioning and other identities) center on campus, thanking me for applying, but letting me know that they would not be able to provide me with a ramp to get up onstage. When I went to inquire as to why this was the case, I was told it was simply impossible. I was so hurt and I pushed them to make it right; going to my university administration to force their hand. Magically, after that, a ramp was procured, and at the time I was the only power wheelchair user who was included in the campus drag show.

This moment made an indelible mark on me that I'll be hard pressed to forget, because it showed me quite clearly that ableism in the queer community was very real, and very much alive. Even though I wheeled up on that stage as Eloise Cum-quat and crip-synched for my life, if you will, I was also sent a strong message that I didn't belong and wasn't truly welcome in queer spaces.

The drag queen on the dancefloor, and my gay bar experiences

Another example of how ableism has directly impacted my queer crippled identity also happened while I was in college. I was so eager to experience the quick, easy queer sexuality that I had seen on TV shows like *Queer as Folk* and other iconic queer offerings of the early 2000s, that I was about ready to burst. Because of this, almost every weekend I went to a bar not far from campus. I remember there was wheelchair access, but only from the back (I feel like there's a queer joke in there somewhere), so whenever I wanted to go in I had to ask one of the patrons who was outside smoking to flag the bouncer and let them know I'd arrived. He would begrudgingly trundle up the stairs of the club and make small talk while he led me to the back entrance where the elevator was. It was always full of boxes and old garbage, but at the time I was just excited to be in the club at all. Looking back, I understand just how unfair and ableist that was.

I would do this weekend after weekend, hoping that I would meet someone to have the queer experience I so desperately desired. But weekend after weekend I would be met with cold stares from club goers. Sometimes, they would trip over my wheelchair as they drunkenly made their way to the bathroom to pee or hook up, and when they did they'd say stuff like, "Hey, you're in the way." I can remember one guy once remarked to his friend, "This guy is like a piece of furniture, always in the way." They ran off laughing after he said it, but the sting in my ears remains to this day, some 20 years later. Comments like this cemented the feeling in me that my disabled body doesn't belong with queer bodies.

Another example of this that sticks in my mind is one night when I went to the bar, and was asked to leave because of my disability. I showed up like I always did, was let in through the back end of the club, hoping that might be the time I'd meet that special someone. I remember trying to get in on the dance floor, moving my power wheelchair throughout the throngs of shirtless 20-year-olds also in search of a part-time lover for the evening. Amid the thumpa thumpa of early millennial pop music, I felt a tap on my shoulder. For a split second, I wondered if my Prince Charming had come to rescue me and sweep me off my feet (which is funny because as a wheelchair user I am never truly on my feet).

As I turned to see who it was, I was struck by a flash of bright colors as they came into view. Standing in front of me was the drag queen who was running the bar that evening. She was a little tipsy, but very beautiful. I half expected her to offer me a quippy comment on my looks or outfit, like most drag queens are known to do, but instead she said, "Honey, would you mind leaving the dance floor. People have said that you're getting in the way of their dancing." I remember being absolutely flabbergasted, so surprised at what she said that for a moment I was unable to move, staring at her, unsure of what to do next. *Did she just ask me to leave because I am disabled?*

At the time, I wasn't the fierce advocate I am today, so I didn't stand up for myself. I remember feeling hot, fighting back the urge to cry, knowing that something ableist had happened to me, but not really having the language to communicate or contextualize it yet. I turned out of the bar, my wheelchair squeaking as the wheels crunched on plastic beer cups, motioning angrily for the bouncer to take me up in the elevator. I was so, so angry that I wasn't included, that my disability had bumped up against my queerness so abruptly in this moment. Why wasn't there room for me?

The pity fuck
Probably the most pivotal moment wherein my queer and crippled identities collided was the first time I ever had sex. I was 19, and I had just moved away from home to my university town. Everyone around me was exploring with dating and sexuality, doing the things that young kids do when they are away from home the very first time. I wanted all the same things, and so every night when I would come home from class, I'd get on my computer and go to gay chat sites in an effort to quench my thirst. I had no idea how to do this—how do you ask someone to come over and fuck you? And how do you let them know that you are severely disabled? I would always send messages like, "Hello. How are you? Would you like to hang out some time?" Very polite and cordial, but they never garnered much of a response.

One night my roommate saw me doing this and he wheeled

his way past me and said, "You're doing it all wrong." He grabbed my keyboard and quickly typed, "I want a blowjob" on the screen. "There, that should get you what you are looking for." I was mortified, but secretly happy that someone else had taken the plunge for me. Within minutes my screen was flush with alerts from potential playmates agreeing to give me the sexual release I longed for. As I clicked through the messages, I came across one guy (okay, there's definitely a pun in there) who looked good. I remember that he had broad shoulders and a big smile that I quite liked. We chatted for a few minutes confirming the plans, the location and our likes and dislikes for the session. Within all of that I remember asking him something like, "I'm disabled—is that okay for you?" Even 20 years later, I still ask this kind of question when I am hooking up with a guy—further evidence that ableism will always be my secret bedfellow.

His answer to this question was simply, "Yup, no problem at all." A rush of relief came over me. "Whew, I don't have to worry, he's okay with my disability." About 30 minutes later, after I had played Christina Aguilera's "Dirty" about 15 times in anticipation of this encounter, he arrived. As he entered my room I was full of nerves; my mouth dry, and I couldn't stop staring at this beautiful man that I was actually going to be with. As he got close to me and kissed me, my body trembled, and having never really done it before, I replicated the hungry kisses that I had seen on my computer screen, as I secretly watched porn at 16. This beautiful man lifted me onto my bed, and I couldn't wait to finally do the things with this guy. He started taking off my clothes, kissing down my disabled body, that, until now, had only ever been naked to be cleaned. All of the different sensations coursing through my body were electric. All I could think was, "I hope my disability doesn't scare him away." Quicker than I would have liked, my body burst into climax, writhing in both joy and embarrassment that I had finished so quickly. My partner looked at me and said, "Oh, okay," watching as I finished.

After a few minutes of us lying there in silence, I said, "So, when can we go on our date?" You see, in my inexperience and naivety I thought that once you made someone cum you were boyfriends with them. I had wanted the sweet, innocent dates I had seen in shows like *Gilmore Girls*, where everything was simple, peaceful and easy, and I truly believed that was what happened next. Oh, was I mistaken. My partner looked at me sheepishly and said, "Oh, no. I don't want to date you. I just came by to help you out because I felt bad for you. You were just a pity fuck."

I could not believe what he had just said. *A pity fuck?* Why would someone say that to me? Was I that bad, or that unattractive, that all I warranted was pity? For years, I had fantasized about how this would come together (ironically, we did not come together). I imagined being liked, licked and lusted over, but pitied...never.

This was the moment when ableism and queerness unequivocally came together in my life. It sliced through me like a hot knife going through butter, and the feeling has sat stuck in my gut ever since. Twenty years later, whenever I am intimate with someone, I worry that they are not with me out of desire but instead out of obligation, because I am severely disabled. I worry that I am seen as a project for them to complete, rather than a person. His words—pity fuck—reverberate in my head whenever I get close to someone, and they are whispered back to me at night when I am alone.

Each of the encounters of ableism that I have outlined here could be seen as simply one incident. One moment in time. A young non-disabled person learning about disability, not meaning to hurt anyone along the way; and, yes, I believe that many of these were not *meant* to be harmful, they were not intended to hurt me as a queer disabled person. Unfortunately, each of these moments has profoundly impacted how I see myself as a queer disabled person, and now I want to share with you how my internalized ableism plays a role in my queer disabled identity.

How my internalized ableism impacted my queer disabled identity

When I first encountered ableism from within the 2SLGBTQ+ community, my instinct was to push it down or bury it. I would convince myself that it was simply a one-off; and if I just kept trying, being persistent in showing this community that I deserved to take up space with them, someone would eventually see me as the cool, sexy disabled guy that I wanted to be viewed as. But, if I'm honest, that persistence never really paid off for me. I would continue to go out to the bar and be rejected or looked at as if I had done something wrong, just by being in their presence. I would continue to go on the apps in search of connection and companionship, only to be questioned about my disability status.

Soon this feeling wasn't just an outward one. All of the

messages, both implicit and explicit, were seeping into who I was as a person—and making me not like myself or my body. I would tell myself that no one wanted to be with me *because* I am disabled. I would (and sometimes still do) compare and contrast my disabled body—curved and crumpled in a power wheel-chair—to the Instagram-ready queer men that I see online, and think, "Nobody wants my body. Who would want a body like this? Who wants to be with a disabled person like me?" This narrative of negativity and internalized ableism has followed me everywhere when I think about being queer and disabled.

If I'm talking to friends about kids or starting a family, I might jokingly remark that, "I'll be alone forever because I am disabled." Sadly, it isn't even a joke, really. If you live in Canada, Australia, the United States or the U.K. and you rely on social assistance benefits, you may lose them if you live with a partner, marry or cohabitate.[3] The idea of going on a date immediately makes me sweaty; not because I'm so excited about the prospect of a coupling, but because I have crippling anxiety around the ableism, discomfort and disclosure I'll have to endure throughout.

When I was younger, the idea of going clubbing was an exhilarating prospect to try again, but as I near 40 now, it feels like a fight for accessibility and inclusion in a space that doesn't want to make the effort. I remember one time, a few years back, there was a big queer party at a new club in the city and I wanted to go. I called up the venue about a week before the event and asked, "Is the venue wheelchair accessible?" The

3   Saunders, M. (2023, March 31). *The Right to Marry: Barriers to intimacy for persons with disabilities.* Harvard Law School Project on Disability. https://hpod.law.harvard.edu/news/entry/right-to-marry.

voice on the other end of the line paused and said, "Yeah, but your power wheelchair might be too big. Do you think you can just get another wheelchair for the evening?" I was so surprised by his response, because what he asked was just like asking an ambulatory person if they could just bring another pair of legs for the evening. Moments like this one have made me far more comfortable alone in my disabled skin; knowing that at least in my aloneness I won't be assaulted by ableism from a community that so loudly preaches "love is love," but quietly agrees that disabled people don't belong here.

One of the other ways that my internalized ableism has impacted my queer identity is far less public and much more private. When I am in the bedroom with a new partner, I find it difficult to enjoy sexual contact, not because I don't love sex, but because I worry that my disabled body is both simultaneously not enough for them and too much for them, all at once. Believe me when I share that that fear is a heavy one to carry with me to the bedroom, and it does make my pursuit of pleasure all the more difficult to navigate.

I bring forward all these personal accounts to make a connection for you about ableism and discrimination against queer disabled folks in the community by community members—it is very real. Ableism has very real consequences that queer cripples like myself still hold on to daily. It isn't simply a buzz word that we can couch alongside other isms in our diversity, equity and inclusion seminars. I said at the beginning of this chapter that I think we keep the way ableism affects queer disabled people in the dark. It is my hope that sharing these stories will help you bring your experiences of queerness, disability and ableism into the light.

CHAPTER 2

What to Do When They Say, "I Don't Do People in Wheelchairs"

How to Use Self-Care Through Ableist
Microaggressions and Keep Queer Crip Joy

want you to imagine for a moment that you are hanging
out on your phone, scrolling through TikToks and YouTube
videos that make you smile, or just procrastinating from
doing that really important thing you have to do. As you're
doing all of this, you decide to take your chances on a dating app. You click on the app and start swiping through your
potential matches. They're all pretty cute; some quirky, some
thirsty, some more serious, but eventually one of them catches
your eye. He's broad shouldered, tall with a well-trimmed beard
and a cheeky smile that reminds you of Jim Halpert from *The
Office* (who wouldn't wanna go on a date with a John Krasinski
lookalike?).

So, you click, and send him your standard, "Hey! Just
thought you were kind of cute. Thought you should know"
message. He starts chatting you up, and after a few rounds
of back and forth, you think that you might like to see him

outside the little square on your phone. For a split second, you imagine what he smells like, and what he looks like with his clothes off. You snap back to reality when you hear the ding on your phone, poised and ready to respond...until you see what he texts. Your eyes widen as you read it: "That would be really cool, but I don't think it would work because...I don't do guys in wheelchairs." Your heart sinks just a little, not because what he said was shocking or really that rude, but because you know what this is—you have dealt with this many times before.

In this chapter, using my own experiences with microaggressions as a queer cripple, I am going to help you with some pro crip tips on how to respond when these types of scenarios happen to you in your life. What do you say when someone responds like that? How can you ultimately keep, cultivate and replicate queer crip joy? But, I'm also gonna go deeper than just tips and tricks. I want to explore with you how those microaggressions make me feel as a disabled person, too. So, let's crack on into it together.

What are microaggressions?

In order to know how to respond to microaggressions properly, it is important to define and discover what microaggressions are. According to an article on the Business Insider website, microaggressions are characterized as "indirect, often unintentional expressions of racism, sexism, ageism, or ableism."[1]

---

1   Ward, M. (2023, July 10). *What Is a Microaggression? 15 things people think are fine to say at work—but are actually racist, sexist, or offensive*. Business Insider. www.businessinsider.com/microaggression-unc onscious-bias-at-work-2018-6.

Now, that is a very broad definition of microaggressions, but it gives you a jumping-off point if you aren't really familiar with the concept (although in the society we live in today, I can't imagine the idea would be entirely novel to you). We've all had someone at the office do something passive aggressive that we didn't like, sending us the subliminal message that we didn't quite belong. How many times have we agonized over an email when someone sends a message that ends, "Best," worrying that they must be plotting our demise at that very moment? Yeah, we've all been there ourselves, and we can all attest to the sinking feeling of dread when something like that happens. But I'd like to suggest that when you are disabled, these little slights—these moments—well, they hit a little differently from most. They're not just little indicators that you don't belong here; no, in fact, they are big, loud, blaring reminders that you are different from everyone else around you. Let me share a few examples from my own life to illustrate this point better for you, friends!

How microaggressions are leveraged against disabled people

"Oh, it is so nice to see you taking care of him"
I remember one time I had invited a friend of mine for dinner one night, and when they got to my house we realized that I was out of the essentials. So, she offered to cook the food for me if I'd buy it. Seeing as I am severely disabled and am basically a hazard in any kitchen, this felt like a grand idea. It was the middle of November, and Instacart wasn't quite a thing just

yet, so we put on 17 layers each (the joys of living in Canada and being a full-time chair user never cease to amaze me) and headed out to the grocery store. When we finally found our way there, chilled to the bone from the cold, we started enthusiastically shopping together and filling our cart up; my friend pushing the cart, while I followed behind, loudly suggesting unnecessary food stuffs to buy.

As all this was happening, an older lady walked up to my friend, who can pass as a non-disabled person, even though she has invisible disabilities herself. The lady tapped my friend on the shoulder, and judging by her age we both immediately prepared to offer any assistance that she might need from us. She turned to my friend and remarked in a soft, sweet voice, "Oh, it's so nice to see you taking care of him in that way. I used to be a nurse, so thank you." At this point, I remember moving my power wheelchair back away from their exchange, subconsciously feeling a pang of ableism at what was happening.

It's kind of funny, because you might think that in moments like this I would be a commanding presence, stopping the ableism at every turn. But, no, I gotta be honest. When people do stuff like this, no matter how well intentioned, I freeze. I am literally unable to stop the ableism in these moments, and that's definitely what happened here. I felt small and hot, while simultaneously noticing the twinge of nervous laughter tickle its way up my throat. Luckily, my friend rebounded without missing a beat. She looked at the lady, and with all the kindness in the world said, "Thank you, but actually he's buying me dinner tonight, so he's taking care of me." The older woman smiled at me, the kind of smile that disabled people are all too used to seeing out in the world. It is a smile that sits squarely between pity and sadness, and every single time I go out of my house, whether I am going for a walk in the summer or zipping out to meet a friend for coffee, I can literally guarantee that I will receive this smile in some variation. It's as if the person doesn't quite understand what their mouths are meant to be doing as they look at this disabled person. Should they smile because he's out of the house, or should they frown because he's out of the house? Regardless, the smile ends up being a unique amalgamation of these two competing emotions. Anyway, she smiled at me like that and went about her day, while my friend and I made a meal out of what just happened, while we continued to shop.

"I don't see you in your wheelchair... I just see you"

Another clear example of the microaggressions that many disabled people face on a daily basis happened to me a couple years back. I had been hired by a big firm to do a presentation on queerness and disability. For me, this was old hat; a persona that I am quite deftly able to slip in and out of. I built my career on telling my truth as a queer disabled person, and I have been lucky enough to be able to get a few bucks here and there by presenting my story for equity and inclusion weeks. I was sure that this time would be no different from all the rest. I put on a nice polo shirt, made sure I was as presentable and professional as a severely disabled person can get (I live in constant fear that if I don't look presentable I will fall into the stereotype of the unkempt disabled person; wow, there is so much internalized ableism to unpack right there) and started my presentation.

It was going swimmingly, and I was easing into my usual cadences about sex and disability, making sure to add little queer crip quips throughout to keep the audience entertained, and keep the nerves that jutted out of the subject of sex and disability at bay. It worked. They laughed when I needed them to, and thought pensively about what I was saying, as if on cue. Perfect! Just as the presentation was wrapping up and I opened the floor for questions (I always expect that one or two nervous folk who aren't sure if their query will be offensive or not will chime in here) a man from the back piped up. He came at me with a big, welcoming smile and said, "Thank you so much for your presentation. You know, as I was watching you up here, more and more, I noticed that I didn't see your wheelchair. I just saw you." I was a little stunned as he said this to me in a room full of his colleagues. I was surprised because I had just spent the better part of two hours sharing stories from my queer disabled life, stories that made it crystal clear that I was very, very disabled.

I watched this man from the back of the room say this to me with his bright smile, and for a split second I was unsure what to do next. I knew that he was coming from a genuine place of support and kindness so I didn't want to admonish him—I had to keep him smiling. But in my mind's eye, I wanted to say, "Did you just hear any of what I just said to you, sir? Do you realize how hard it is for me to sit in this wheelchair day in and day out, something that I have to navigate and think about constantly, just for you to tell me that you don't even see it?! Some days I hate my wheelchair, but at least I know it's there. What do you mean you can't see the 300lb contraption that I am sat in, sir?!" Naturally, I didn't say any of this to the man. I smiled just as widely as him and said, "Thank you so much for saying that. I know where you are coming from, but it is okay to see my wheelchair." I could see the sheepish look on his face, as though he had done something wrong. I reassured him he hadn't—that it was a learning experience for him—took my pay and left, hoping that anything I had said about being really, really disabled had stuck with the others in the room.

This particular instance wasn't so much that I didn't belong in the room with them, but rather that I couldn't belong with them in the room as the full-on disabled person that I am. It didn't make me feel small exactly, but it did leave me with a sense of wonder over how I was perceived by others out in the world, and thanks to that interaction, it's something that I still think about from time to time. Do you see me as the disabled person I know that I am, or do you only see me as a version of a disabled person that you need me to be so that you can feel okay with me?

"Are you lost?" and, "It's so good to see you out—good for you!"

Other types of microaggressions around my disability that I have received have been weirdly random. Every day in the summer, I go outside to a big park across the street from my apartment. Honestly, I am so glad that it is there because it definitely helps with my mental health. When it's warm out, I take a podcast of choice with me (usually about paranormal stuff or murder) and slowly wheel around the park, listening to the sounds of summer around me, kids playing, parents screaming at the kids to stop playing, and occasionally a really sexy shirtless runner will jog on by.

One such afternoon, I went outside for my usual jaunt. As I was driving my chair past a woman walking on the pathway, I heard, "Excuse me, sir, are you lost?" I kept going, thinking that clearly this couldn't be directed at me. Perhaps she was a parent talking to her son in that playful adultlike way parents do with toddlers. I kept going, but her question cut through my murder pod again, "Sir, excuse me, are you lost?" This time there was no mistaking it, she was talking to me. I turned to look, still hoping that a bewildered child that she was in charge of would pop up somewhere. No such luck. She looked at me, a sense of concern stamped across her features, "Are you lost?" she repeated. I smiled at her and very quickly replied, "No, thank you, no." She nodded and continued on her way, and I cut the other way across the accessible path to continue listening to my murder podcast. I tried to listen to the story in my headphones, but I was struck by something that was niggling in the back of my mind. If I had actually needed help, the chances are that the woman would have ignored me and kept walking.

It has happened to me a dozen or so times over the years. I'll have dropped a hat or my mittens, and people will just pretend that I, in my 300lb wheelchair (the one you literally have to close your eyes not to see me in), don't exist. But when I am out there in the world, suddenly I am a problem to be solved. I must be lost, because why would someone like me be outside without any supervision? It's funny how that works, isn't it?

Another pretty common microaggression that most disabled people experience is this one. I was out at a gay club a few years ago. I had just moved closer to my hometown from university, and I wanted to immerse myself in queerness (read: I wanted to immerse myself in dick). I decided to go to this big gay party where some porn star would be on a Friday night just before Fall kicked in. This was a critical time for a wheelchair-using queer like myself, because once the snow starts to fall, I basically turn into a "bear in a chair." I mean that in the sexually suggestive coy way that you just read it, and a literal one. Winter makes it inevitably harder to go out in the snow in my wheelchair, and I'm also waiting for transit, and waiting on attendant care workers to get me dressed appropriately, and so on. I end up hibernating from October until the end of March, only really leaving the house for the holidays and that weird in-between time that falls from December 26 to January 4.

I knew that I had to take this opportunity and run with it. So, I booked a disability transit bus that would take me three hours to get into the city if I was lucky, and planned to have a relatively okay night, most likely being ignored by my community. When I got there, the thumpa thumpa of the bass had already started. As I filed in behind guys who looked way better than my crumpled, crippled body, I nervously scanned the room to see if I knew anyone. There were a few guys that I had seen on the apps, and we nodded silently at one another to signal that we recognized each other, but there wasn't anyone I'd call a friend in the room.

Maybe about an hour later, I heard someone say, "Oh, hi!" Naturally, I had taken the position that with all the hotties in the room, I wasn't the one they were speaking to. Suddenly, I felt a tap on my shoulder. This really sweet club kid with big brown eyes and a big smile knelt down next to my wheelchair to talk to me. I always brace myself when someone automatically kneels down to chat with me because I know maybe they are trying to be accessible, but also, you don't have to kneel, really. He said, "It's so nice to see you out here. Are you enjoying your night?"

Now, it wasn't what he said that irked me; what he had asked was a pretty standard question for a bar night, one that anyone could expect to get, right? It was more how he asked me the question—a slow, deliberate tone in his voice, signaling to me that he wasn't sure I understood what was happening. I smiled and answered him politely, "Oh yeah, great night." I very quickly put on my educational cap and answered questions about my wheelchair, my cerebral palsy, and many others. It wasn't that I necessarily wanted to, but he was one of the only people who engaged me all night, so answering questions that I could rattle off without thinking was better than being ignored.

The stories that I share above are types of microaggressions that disabled people deal with every single day. Because they are so common for so many of us, we have learned how to deal with them in one way or another. We smile and say something empowering to counteract the ableism, or, if you're me, sometimes you just giggle at the true absurdity of it all, even when you don't mean to. Every disabled person has some kind of story that brings these microaggressions into focus and each of us has our own way of dealing with them, and we often share these stories together.

How microaggressions are leveraged against queer disabled people

While every disabled person has a story about how they handled an everyday ableist microaggression, some of the things that we don't have enough of, I think, are stories about how these ableist microaggressions are used in queer spaces against queer disabled folk. When the microaggression takes place among queer people, I have to note that, at least in my experience, it becomes much more pointed and full of spikes. Gone are the cute little old ladies in the grocery story praising a friend for helping me; they have been replaced by queer people who are judging me for even wanting to be there. Allow me to share some examples of this.

"Does your dick work?"

I can't tell you how excited I was when I first started using queer-centered sex apps like Grindr or Scruff (it's just like Grindr but for guys with beards and tattoos and bellies). It was as if a whole new world had opened up for me, and suddenly all my worries about the accessibility of a physical space didn't feel so big. Now I could just "point, click, dick," right? It was awesome to see all the possibilities of playmates that were open to me. I started chatting quite eagerly, trying to arrange hookups and fuck buds on the daily. I had fun honing my queer online persona, finding ways to weave my wheeled identity into the space. Sometimes I'd be Cripple X, other times, Big Dick Cripple or some variation of that. It was a great way for me to unleash so much pent up energy and merge my disability and desire in one place. This was really important to me because, like so many of you queer crips reading this, my sexuality is deleted from so many narratives, but here I could make it my own.

I was having all this fun until I noticed a recurring theme that often accompanied my online interactions, and it was becoming increasingly hard to ignore. I would digitally sidle up next to a guy who I thought was cute (typically bearded, bright eyes, etc.) and I would start chatting him up. Almost immediately following introductions, he would open with, "So, I have a question...does it work?" I didn't really have to ask him what he was talking about, because I knew that he was asking if my genitals worked. It was (and still is) so jarring to experience this, because your whole personhood is reduced to your genitalia's ability to perform. But, it's even worse than that. Because you have been upfront that you are deliciously disabled, there is a looming misconception that because you are disabled you must be paralyzed (because we all know that's the only way to be disabled, right?) and because you are paralyzed you must not be able to have erections.

When I was younger, and honestly less connected to the ways in which I too could perpetuate ableism, I would say something like, "Don't worry, it works just fine" or, "At least my dick works!" I wanted them to see that I was just like them in that regard; that I could do just what they were doing—I could be as gay and as virile as them, without a problem. As I got older and kept getting asked this question every single time I was on the apps, I finally realized just how ableist it was. Looking back on it now I think to myself, "And, if my genitals didn't work the way you expected them to, did that mean that I was not worthy of intimacy and affection? If I couldn't get an erection or stay hard, was I no longer worthy of your attention?"

One of the great things about being disabled is our ability to adapt pleasure into whatever works for us, and it is shameful that the queer male, penis-having community is so quick to measure your worth via your genitals. Every time I get one of these questions on the app, I compare myself to others out there, and it becomes harder and harder (no penis pun intended there) to love my disabled body and what I bring to the table. It feels as if I have lost before I've started, and that can be really hard to reconcile.

"I don't do guys in wheelchairs"

One time I was on the apps and I was chatting with a guy at 3am. I'll admit I wasn't after a long-term thing in this moment; rather, I wanted some company for an hour or two. I figured that since that's kind of how these apps are designed anyway, I'd shoot my shot. This guy was cute, quick witted and seemed down to come over. The bright blue light from my iPhone illuminated my room, as I lay in bed and we traded dirty pictures and made plans. About halfway through our conversation, it became clear that he hadn't realized I was a wheelchair user, so I said, "You know I am in a wheelchair. You're okay with that, yeah?"

As quickly as our text bubbles had flown back and forth five minutes earlier detailing our desire, it was at this moment that they abruptly ended. "Oh," he replied. I stared at the familiar chat bubbles as they continuously faded and then reappeared while I waited for a response. I knew that some variation of a rejection was being crafted, but I was entirely unprepared for what he actually typed. "I don't do guys in wheelchairs" popped up in the bubble. It took me a second to process what he was telling me and in that moment all the excitement left me like a birthday party balloon slowly deflating. I felt angry and simultaneously jealous of able-bodied people and those who didn't need to think about a wheelchair every day. I wanted to send a witty quip back to him, something that showed him his remark wasn't bothersome to me. Something like, "Well, actually I'd be in bed, so..." but I didn't bother. Instead, I turned off the phone letting the darkness of my room envelop me—in that moment I felt safest being alone, not worrying about dating, especially if this was the kind of thing that I would have to deal with every time I made an attempt.

"I don't think I would enjoy myself"

I remember once I had the chance to get to know a queer porn star. We were talking about queer disabled sex, what I found hot about it and so on, and it was all going quite well. I asked him if he ever thought about doing a scene with a disabled person like me. I was hoping he'd play it coy and keep the possibility open, but without missing a single beat he said, "No, I don't think I would enjoy myself." I was taken aback by this honest admission from someone I looked up to (and if I'm honest got off to), but I steeled myself and asked him, "Why not?" As easily as he had before he said, "There's just so much you can't really do that I like." I tried my hardest to remain cool and casual, but had you really looked at me in that moment, you would have seen the hurt in my eyes. His comment stung the most because he had forced me to confront a feeling that I often held within myself as a sexually active disabled person, and that is: "I can't give people pleasure because I am disabled." I kept the end of our interaction light and breezy, but this confirmation that I wasn't really good enough has held fast ever since.

"Oh, I am so sorry that happened to you/Google says you…"

Sometimes when I let the cute boy on the app know that I am disabled and use a wheelchair, I get an immediate response.

The chat bubbles will be swift, and for a split second I will brim with excitement that perhaps, this time, things will be different. But, of course, that excitement is short-lived because what he types next leaves a pit in my tummy that is the size of the Grand Canyon. "Oh, I'm so sorry that happened to you... awwww." I never quite understand what to do when they say stuff like that. It feels different for me because, at least in my case, nothing happened. There was no big, tragic life-changing moment where I transformed from able-bodied to disabled. There wasn't a moment where I had all the privilege of able-bodiedness and it was suddenly stripped from me without warning, nothing like that. I was born with cerebral palsy—it is part of my DNA—it is in my bones; every cell in my body, every muscle is infused with it. It isn't something that happened, it's just something that is. So, when guys online immediately assume that I am paralyzed, it's hard to know what to do next. Do I feed into their pity so that I can access intimacy, or do I correct them right away?

I remember one time I was chatting with a potential hookup on the apps in Toronto. I let him know that I had a disability, and he asked which one. I was feeling confident so I said cerebral palsy. Right after I told him, he disappeared from the chat for about two hours. I assumed he ghosted me—nothing to worry about—on to the next. When he finally returned, I was ready to set up our playtime. Very abruptly he came back with, "I read up about what you have. Google says that you have seizures, can't talk and can't think for yourself. So...I don't think we can hook up." I was pretty angry that a cursory Google search stopped him from seeing me—from knowing me—from wanting to at least fucking try.

All of these examples I have shared have shaped how I understand my disabled queerness. These types of microaggressions from within the queer community have cut me to the core of who I am. They have embedded themselves in the depths of my palsied personhood, and have forever altered my relationship with others. And myself.

Where do these everyday microaggressions about disability come from?

Now, I am no social scientist, but I am curious to understand where these microaggressions come from. Why are we so quick to treat disabled people with kid gloves or like they are less than? Let's quickly explore this together.

As far back as the Middle Ages, disabled people were thought to be possessed by the Devil, or an evil spirit. Because of this, they were not offered care or help.[2] I have read stories about young children with disabilities from these time periods who died because their parents believed that they were changelings or faeries sent to harm the family. Moving forward in time, disability was inextricably linked to eugenics in the 1800s, as racism, classism and ableism fueled the drive for the "perfect race" of people.[3] You may be thinking, "But Andrew, this was hundreds of years ago, things must have changed for the better, right?" I can say that after hundreds of years things

---

2   Resnick, A. (2023, July 7). *Ableism: What It Means, History, Types, Examples, How It's Harmful*. Verywell Mind. www.verywellmind.com/what-is-ableism-5200530.

3   Resnick, A. (2023, July 7). *Ableism: What It Means, History, Types, Examples, How It's Harmful*. Verywell Mind. www.verywellmind.com/what-is-ableism-5200530.

have changed, yes. We have laws for disabled people and way more accessibility than we did previously. The Americans with Disabilities Act 1990, and similar statutes, propelled our understanding of disability forward.

But despite all this progress for disabled people, one of the things that hasn't really changed is the attitude of people around disability. In my opinion, we haven't really given the everyday person the opportunity to confront and grapple with their own ableism. Non-disabled people need to be given the opportunity to say, "Disability scares the absolute shit out of me. What can I do about that?" It is my belief that until we start having those uneasy conversations—and doing so without shame and blame—nothing much will move forward. Moreover, due to a lack of accessibility that persists, even in the modern tech-filled landscape we know today, and because non-disabled people rarely see us out in the world, they are not given real-world, tangible examples of disabled people. They don't see us in the dance clubs or on the Pride floats in June, dancing and laughing with everyone else. Because of this invisibility, a mysterious lore, one full of half-truths and misconceptions, is codified via the court of public opinion as fact, and the disabled microaggression is given new life—one that has spanned generation after generation.

Disabled sexuality and its link to microaggressions from LGBTQ+ people

Alongside looking at the history of ableism in general, and how it has shaped the way we view disabled bodies, it is also critically important to explore some of the history around disabled sexuality. I want to do this to understand how and why the queer community often feels so rife with ableism, and particularly why their microaggressions cut as deep as they do.

The history of disabled sexuality is full of examples of ableism and ideologies that support the belief that disabled people are worthless. An example of this belief comes from the eugenics movement, started in the 1800s as "it sought to control the reproduction of those considered unfit. Namely, people who had physical and social disorders and traits associated with the poor, such as alcoholism, habitual criminality, prostitution, diseases, epilepsy and 'feeble-mindedness.'"[4]

As we can see from the above quote, the idea that disabled people should not have a sexuality is not new. It has roots, which, over many years have taken hold, twisting and turning the idea of disabled sexuality into a scary thing and something that we all must avoid. Something that we mustn't think or speak of because it is bad and wrong. Therefore, sexually active disabled people must be wrong too. I also think that these sexual microaggressions against disabled people come out because queer society at large never sees solid representations of queer disabled sexuality.

In January 2022, I was given the opportunity to film as part of the *Queer as Folk* reboot. The scene that I had been asked to participate in was a disabled sex party scene. I remember getting on set and seeing a bunch of disabled people ready to

---

4   Moghaddami, A. (2021, November 15). *UK Disability History Month: Laws, Relationships and Sex* [Review of UK Disability History Month: Laws, Relationships and Sex]. Parliamentary Archives: Inside the Act Room. https://archives.blog. parliament.uk/2021/11/15/uk-disability-history-month-laws-relationships-and-sex.

shoot the scene; wheelchair users in leather harnesses, power chair users in sexy lingerie, people with amputations looking hot as fuck. It was incredible because I'd never seen anything like that. As we shot the scene over and over again, me in a patient lift pretending to make sex faces as a severely queer cripple, I was overcome with emotion because disabled people were being seen as sexual beings here and that was fucking groundbreaking.

After hours of shooting, when we finally wrapped, the director stopped me to tell me that I had been part of television history for disabled people, and I was so proud, while also feeling angry that this type of queer crippled representation wasn't really anywhere else. I think that a lot of the disability microaggressions occur because non-disabled queer people don't know what to say or what to do around a disabled person. Maybe if they did, they'd actually see us as sexually viable.

Another reason I feel there are a lot of sexually ableist microaggressions that queer disabled people have to put up with from inside the community, particularly in my case the gay male community, is the fear of illness and sickness as a holdover from the height of the AIDS crisis. When someone was diagnosed with AIDS/HIV, their bodies would resemble that of a sick/disabled person—someone unable to perform the requirements of masculinity and desirability that have become cornerstones of queer male hookup culture.[5] This makes a lot of sense regarding my own experiences, and the microaggressions I have shared. When they notice me in my big

5   Hrynyk, N. (2021). "No sorrow, no pity": Intersections of disability, HIV/AIDS, and gay male masculinity in the 1980s. *Disability Studies Quarterly*, 41(2). https://doi.org/10.18061/dsq.v41i2.7148.

power wheelchair with my big dorky smile, spindly legs, curved spine, spastic jumps, and all the things that make me the queer disabled cutie I am, it jams up their perception, which is full of white, able-bodied muscular men. So when I come into view, they haven't a clue where to go or what to do. They want to know if my genitals work because they want to stay as close within the lines of acceptable queerness, and if my dick works, that's something they know how to navigate.

It's helpful to understand for myself that even though their microaggressions towards me have been beyond hurtful in ways that have forever deepened my own fears around my sexual worth (so many new fears unlocked, thanks guys!), it isn't necessarily malicious intent that's driving them—it's fear. They are just afraid. The irony is that while they're afraid of saying something wrong, doing the wrong thing, or not having me meet some fictitious queer sex standard they've been fed by community members, I am just as scared as they are.

What do we do when these microaggressions happen?

Let's take a minute here and explore what we can do as queer cripples when these microaggressions from within our community happen. I know the easiest answer is, "When a queer community member asks you if your junk works, tell them to fuck off." Yup, you could do that, and I completely understand the impulse to do it. Trust me, I've had a lot of those moments, and I'm certain that I'll have many more. For me though, I think there's more nuance in it than that. I don't want to push my queer community members away; I want to find a way to let them into my experience, while letting the anger go. You should know that I have in no way perfected this part of the journey, but let me try at least to offer you some ways to get through the anger that help you retain that queer crip joy.

Take a nap in your mobility device

One of the things that helps me to brush off the ableism that I deal with from within my community is, believe it or not, a good fucking nap in my wheelchair. After you read the next microaggression on Tinder and it pisses you off to the point where you want to throw your phone across the room, I want you to stop for a minute and take a deep breath. Put your phone on Do Not Disturb, close your eyes and drift off in your wheelchair. I can't tell you how many times the ableism just stings really badly from a guy saying something insensitive, and a 2pm afternoon nap fixes me right up. It doesn't always take the pain away, but it does remind me to slow down and stop focusing so much on them. It gives me time to appreciate my disabled body and my disabled space in the world.

Talk to other disabled folks

There is a scene in the Netflix documentary *Crip Camp* where a bunch of the disabled campers start talking to each other about some of the challenges they encounter, and it is by far one of my favorite things to see on film. What I love about it is the fact that they are sharing these thoughts together; and I think queer crip community is so important. If you need to find queer crip joy in those tough moments when someone on the apps has been particularly hurtful, bring these issues to your community members. Whether that be digitally or in person, having those conversations with others who have experienced it, in only the ways queer disabled people have, is so important.

I remember once I was talking to a guy on the apps who lived about 8,000 kilometers away (so nothing was going to happen anyway). I messaged him that he was cute and he responded with the puke emoji. A few minutes later, he messaged me: "Why would I be with you?" It really hurt, and in a flash of upset, I posted it to my social media, because I wanted people to see what it was we deal with. Within minutes, I was flooded with messages from other disabled folks telling me that they had had similar experiences, and that they understood what it felt like to deal with this. That was so affirming to me, and it really, really helped remind me that I was not alone by any means. Give it a try yourself—finding community in those moments is better than going it alone.

Tell them how it makes you feel

One of the very best ways to find my queer crip joy in those instances where my palsy pride has been wounded is to lean into the honesty with the person who said this hurtful thing to you. I don't mean in a decidedly Instagrammable post that makes you look saucy; no, I mean genuinely explaining to them how the ableism they have levied against you impacts you. Don't do it with any anger or expectation (this is a whole lot harder than it sounds), but just let them know. Putting that knowledge out into the world helps me retain queer crip joy because maybe, just maybe, what I've said will turn on the lightbulb for them and plant the seeds so that they can start looking at their role in ableism a little differently. And if not, at least you were honest.

Far too often we minimize these feelings so that we as disabled queer folk can be palatable, but we don't have to do that—at least not all the time.

Ask them how they might feel when it is their turn

One of the best ways to cultivate queer crip joy in those moments, at least for me, is to turn the tables just a little bit. So, when that cute Jim Halpert lookalike is about to go down on you, the heat from your bodies rising, and he asks, "Uh, hey, do your genitals work?" I want you to stop him and ask him how, when it is him sat in that wheelchair, exposed and vulnerable, he will feel being asked that question. Will he worry he isn't sexy? Or worry that he isn't good enough? Remind him that when it is his turn to be disabled (because that's coming), these kinds of questions will hurt him too. It brings me the smallest sliver of queer crip joy (not wishing disability on anyone, of course) watching them realize in real-time that they may well be in my position soon enough. They will be just as disabled, and they will go through it too.

As the realization that he can become disabled at any time flickers across his face, you can smile and say, "Don't worry, Jim, unlike you, I will do guys in wheelchairs."

CHAPTER 3

"How to Have the Best Queer Cripple Sex of Your Life"

O h, boy, this chapter was one of the hardest things I've ever had to start writing. Usually when I write a piece about disability it doesn't take me too long to get into a rhythm. I've been writing about sex, disability and queerness for a few years now, and I have learned how to make it digestible and accessible to an audience. For this one though, if I'm honest, I feel like a big imposter. How can I give you, dear reader, advice on having the best sex of your life as a disabled person when I feel like I haven't really had the best sex of my life yet as a disabled person?! I feel kind of fraudulent here. The truth is that even though I make most of my living talking about sexuality and disability as a disability awareness consultant, I don't have a lot of sex (I know, what a shock).

More often than not, I spend my time convincing people that severely disabled people such as myself are valuable and worthy as sexual and romantic partners. The more and more I do this work, the less I actually get to engage in any kind of pleasure with people. I often don't get to unleash the dirty, disabled seated slut that lives inside my body and that has been extremely frustrating. Can you imagine writing and talking about sexuality and disability day in and day out, urging people to see you as a sexual being, but then when the opportunity arises, nothing actually happens because people are afraid? That's pretty much how my work on sexuality and disability has panned out, and this truth makes it difficult for me to feel as though I am any kind of authority figure in this field.

I see other queer sex educators without disabilities sharing their stories of romantic trysts and orgies and sex parties every weekend, and it makes me pretty angry that I don't have the same wealth of knowledge to give you pearls of palsied wisdom. It makes me angry that some of the best sex that I have ever had has been paid for. I love and respect sex workers, and I am very privileged and very lucky to be able to access them when I need to. Moreover, I am eternally grateful for some of the relationships that being a client to male sex workers has afforded me. But, I would be lying if I didn't tell you that as a disabled person, one who has a body that often makes other queer men retreat in fear (I'm not kidding. I've actually had hookups where the guy retreated in fear, running away from my wheelchair), it breaks my heart that most of the good sex I have had has been transactional. That is a gut punch to my soul, and I won't pretend otherwise.

Because of all these things, and the fact that I am really, really disabled, it feels as if I can't really give you tips on how to have the greatest crippled sex of your life... But, fuck it, I am going to do my best to try in this chapter. I am going to share with you stories that have made having the "best sex" as a disabled person very difficult for me, while also sprinkling in moments where I almost had great sex as a queer cripple (because I genuinely don't believe that I have had the greatest sex of my disabled life just yet). In this chapter, I want to dive into what my fantasy of sex and disability looked like, and how that has differed from the reality of the kind of sex that I am able to engage in.

From here, I promise friends, I do want to give you some tips that I have learned to make your sex as a queer disabled person that much better, no matter what it may look like for you. These will be the things that so many of us know to do, but that we rarely see in print or that are readily available to us as a queer disabled community. I want to make them available for all, so that disabled and non-disabled readers alike will have something to reference when they hit the sheets with someone they care about (or, care about just for tonight). So, as I say on my podcast at the start of every episode, "Let's get comfy, cozy and crippled and get started!"

Losing the ability to masturbate: The physical effects of disability on my sexual identity

From the time I was 12 years old, I loved to masturbate. If I am brutally honest, I loved the act of masturbation as a pre-teen, teenager and young adult the most, not necessarily because it felt good, but because in my case as a young disabled person it was one of the only things that I could do, from start to finish, on my own. Everything else, from waking until sleep had to be fully facilitated by another person. If I wanted to scratch my back, get a glass of water, use the washroom, have a shower, or any of those mundanities, I had to call on someone else. They had to be in the room during some of my most vulnerable moments. But when I discovered jerking off, and realized that I didn't need anyone else to pleasure myself, it was like a whole new world opened up for me. Masturbation was the moment I could connect to my queerness and immerse myself in the male-on-male fantasies that lived in my head.

As I formed my queer identity at 16 and 17, I imagined the most beautiful men ravaging my disabled body with reckless abandon. I would wait until my childhood bedroom had been drunk in by the shadows and the light danced on my walls. Once I knew I was alone, I would slowly slide my hand down to my privates. I tried so hard to emulate the masturbatory techniques of the male porn stars I'd watch secretly in the glow of an early 2000s internet connection, but try as I might, my spastic hands wouldn't allow me to pump in the way they did. I wasn't discouraged. I remember lying there each night, finding the perfect position to achieve self-pleasure. Instead of the common pump motion I used to study in secret, I had to craft my own technique. I eventually learned that if I used my thumb along the shaft of my penis, I could achieve unending pleasure despite my palsy. Once I learned to do that, many a night I was able to bring myself to orgasm as a disabled person, and it is something that I cherished as one of the only bastions of my independence.

I wish that I could say that this ability was one that lasted for me, but unfortunately, I can't. Around the time I hit age 31 or 32, the spasticity in my hands resulting from my cerebral palsy was getting worse. I remember trying to pleasure myself at night, waiting for the sounds in my apartment to be just right; and the lighting to be a cozy glow. I would slip my hand between my legs, ready to alleviate all the pressures of my day and slip into a fantasy where Channing Tatum or some other hunky guy took me to exciting depths, only to be met with shooting pains throughout my hands. I did my best to power through those feelings of pain, so that I could enjoy my body, but sooner than I would like to admit to myself, the pain won. I gave up and just stopped trying. The amount of work that I had to do to even get to a place where pleasure was possible felt insurmountable. I don't think that we truly understand or tackle bodily grief enough when we talk about sexuality; and we certainly don't talk about the bodily grief that comes when you are severely disabled and you lose a function that you always thought you would have access to. Let's do that here.

When I stopped self-pleasuring, at first it was to avoid the pain that the cerebral palsy caused my hands. I could justify that for a while, convincing myself that once the pain magically went away, this thing I had control over would come back to me. But then, weeks would go by. Then months. I became increasingly angry with myself and my body. Why, all of a sudden, couldn't I do this thing, this thing that in my head, meant that I was a man (looking back on that now, I see that is chock full of toxic masculinity, but at the time...)? Why did everyone else get to have this thing, except me?

I felt in many ways that I was somehow being punished because I am severely disabled—and that has been, and continues to be, one of the hardest parts of my sexual journey as a disabled person, knowing that my body will not and cannot perform like all the rest. If I'm being completely transparent with you here, the hardest part has been realizing that for an act as intimate, private and loving as masturbation, I now need someone else to help me. Holy shit, that hasn't been easy. Okay, the whole truth is, as a result of that happening I feel two things simultaneously: disconnected from my body and betrayed by my body.

What being disconnected from your severely disabled body actually feels like

It is such a strange feeling when you are severely disabled and not really connected to your body the way that you want to be. The best way that I can describe it to you, if you haven't really experienced it before, is that you just go numb. Your body becomes this thing you have to have taken care of, and nothing else. So, I will let personal support workers touch my body and clean my body every day, and while they do this to me I drift away, thinking of other things or daydreaming about one thing or another. It becomes more and more difficult to look at my body, specifically my genitalia, and derive any kind of pleasure from them. That disconnection feels heavy sometimes; it feels as if I am constantly waiting for someone or something to flip the switch that will put me back in my body with all the vitality that I have, but it never arrives. It's hard, but the bodily betrayal is so much worse.

Bodily betrayal and my experiences

Another big issue that I have with not being able to physically pleasure myself anymore is the bodily betrayal I experience when my body does something that I don't want it to. For me, that is randomly cumming when I don't want to. It is really jarring to be sitting there watching an old episode of *Grey's Anatomy* or working on a project, and all of a sudden experience ejaculation out of the blue. It happens pretty frequently to my disabled body, and I just try to let it go, and recognize that I have no control over it; it is a bodily function, and I have a body. I try to do that, but I cannot shake the truth that I often feel as if my body has betrayed me in this regard. It feels like, "I can't do so many other things, and now I can't even enjoy an orgasm or a climax when and how I want to." I want to scream at my body and say, "This is mine! You cannot take this from me!" but that doesn't really work.

Having issues with bodily betrayal around masturbation, ejaculation and disability has impacted how I think about the sex that I am having as a disabled person. All of these issues, in many ways, have caused me to disconnect from the pleasure altogether, and to question my own desirability within my community as a queer disabled person. I mean, who wants a guy who can't cum when he wants and can't even give a good handjob because his hands don't work, right?

The fantasy of sex and severe disability versus the reality

The fantasy
When I am alone in my head, the fantasies that I have as a disabled person are very different from what is actually happening when I get to engage in a sexual moment. Let me explain. In my head, I imagine that my disability is no issue, and that my object of desire will have no problem taking me out of my wheelchair and devouring me as they wish. I picture clothes being torn, being whisked out of my wheelchair and pleasured

in every way imaginable. I picture my wheelchair as only adding to the excitement and the forbidden nature of the sexual encounter. I imagine that my lover is having the best sex of their lives, because they can't believe that this disabled guy could make them reach the heights of such ecstasy. I can see, in my mind's eye, the joy spread across their face as my disabled body brings them complete sexual satisfaction. Sometimes in my fantasies, I am able to walk and do all the things that I know I can't in real life. I picture myself being dominant, no wheelchair in sight, nothing to denote that I am the "weak one." I can take control here; I can give and receive pleasure without delay. Those fantasies stay with me, and they are often top of mind when I think about hooking up or having a sexual encounter. They help me to keep the ableism that I will deal with in reality at bay, and they are a safe place for me to feel whole as a sexual disabled being. They make me feel wholly myself.

The reality

My reality of sex and disability veers greatly away from the fantasy. I spend most of the time counseling my non-disabled lover on how to be okay with my disabled body. I make sure they are comfy, minimize all parts of my disability in the hope that they won't be scared of me, and reconcile with the truth that this kind of sex for them will most likely be somewhat disappointing because it is not at all what they are used to. The reality is that I often steel myself, bracing for them to say something ableist in the moment or never talk to me again after they leave.

My reality of sex and disability is full of fears, ones that I can't even bring myself to talk about because they are so deeply hidden beneath the confident bravado that I must portray to get any attention in the bedroom at all. The whole experience leaves me doing the mental gymnastics of whether or not I am good enough to even be having sex. As I lie there, my curved crippled body vulnerable, I wonder if my partner is thinking of someone altogether better than me, someone more abled and less needy, worthy of their time.

So, with that reality in mind, and all the above, you're probably thinking to yourself, who the fuck is Andrew to give you any advice whatsoever about the best queer cripple sex of your life? I wanted to show you that just because my name is on this book, I am not an expert lording my knowledge over you. I am just as influenced by ableism, fear and disability erasure as you are. We're all in this together, I promise. So, let me try. Here are some of the ways that I think you can have the best queer crip sex of your life.

How to have the best queer cripple sex of your life

1. Confront your internalized ableism

One of the worst moments of internalized ableism that I have ever experienced was during my second threesome with two workers, one of them the hottest guy I've ever been with in my life. There we were having great sex, two beautiful men on top of me, and all of a sudden I was hit by a huge wave of internalized ableism. I watched them have sex with each other on top of me, watching their bodies move in ways that my crippled body could never. I watched them devour each other, and I just felt that I was there, not truly a worthwhile participant, and holy wow did that hurt. As they tried to include me in the playtime, all I could hear was, *They don't actually want you at all. They just feel bad for you, Andrew. Your disabled body is worthless.* Those whispers reverberated in my head and heart throughout the whole session.

Before you even consider sex with anyone else (or yourself for that matter), I urge you to sit down and have a conversation with yourself around your disabled body. I have so much internalized ableism running through me at any given time, reminding me that I am just not worth anyone's time, it can be hard to quiet that shit. But, I have learned that if I talk to myself about it before a sexual experience, it helps things go a little better. Is that little voice telling you that you aren't sexy? Thank it for its opinion and move forward. Are you worried that your body can't do what others can in the bedroom and you'll disappoint your partner because of your chronic pain? Sit with that feeling for a moment and remind yourself that pain doesn't diminish your disabled value. Do you worry that you'll scare them away? Ask yourself what you are scared of in this situation. It might also help to write down how the internalized ableism makes you feel. Putting those words we say to ourselves as queer cripples down on paper may help you to see that they are untrue and not real at all, and I think it is really important to see a visualization of that.

I also think it is important to unpack where exactly that internalized ableism stems from. Listen to the story you're telling yourself. Is it based in a fear that you won't ever be someone's object of desire (that one is mine)? Is it connected to the fact that every time you try to have sex your body has other plans?

Could it be that you have the ableism from past attempts at sexuality swirling around in your thoughts? Did your family diminish your sexuality because of disability? Trust me when I say I know that these are not easy questions to bring forward, even to yourself, but if you do that, it can start to heal some of the negative thoughts that often join queer disabled folks in the bedroom.

2. Give your partner a chance to unpack their ableism with you

In 2011, I moved into my very first apartment. I had never lived on my own before, and I had a lot of down time. One night at 3am I thought it was the perfect time to get on the apps and invite a random stranger over for intimacy. I made sure that my attendant care workers had put me to bed and I started my search. I met this really cute, young able-bodied guy who agreed to come over. After what felt like an eternity, he knocked on my door. I clicked my big metal automatic door opener, and watched as the slender shadow moved closer and into view. In front of me stood this mid-twenties guy in jeans and a flannel sweater. I offered him a big bright smile, hoping that he'd enter my space so that we could swap head or something. Instead, he sat in the crook of my doorway, not moving at all, save for a trembling hand. Since I was a little boy, I'd known what this look was. He had never really truly been in the presence of a disabled person like me. The precocious boy version of me would know exactly what to do: talk his ear off about how cool my wheelchair is. So, I tried making jokes with him that poked fun at my disability to show him that it wasn't so scary. Nothing worked. He was stone silent, as I prattled on.

Eventually, he whispered, "I'm scared of you." I knew it before he said it, but to hear the words squeak out of him as he clung to my doorway, as if I would lunge at him, was a heart-stopping moment. I remember it vividly because I could have said something catty and cruel to him in that moment. I could have met his honesty with a witty remark like Samantha in *Sex and the City*, and tossed him out on his ear. I decided to take a different approach. As I lay in my bed, I asked him to come closer. I then asked him, "Why are you scared?" He didn't initially answer with words, instead gesturing to all the weird contraptions he saw. The things that I saw as part of my day: my Hoyer lift, my sling, my power wheelchair, my commode chair and so on.

He went on to tell me that he hadn't expected that I should need so much, and that I had shattered his expectations of a quick, easy, non-committal encounter. I've heard this from suitors since, and there really isn't any way to truly soften it. Watching someone realize that you are severely disabled and need things they didn't expect; watching them unpack that in real time is a hard feeling, and there really isn't a word for that.

There was so much in this moment that I wanted to scream at him, so many things I wanted to say that would shut up all the things he was saying. I stayed as quiet as I could, and I just let him get it out. The more he spoke to me, the more I could see his fear of me abate. His shoulders relaxed, his tremble stopped. We didn't end up having sex, but I remember that he curled his body around mine and we just cuddled together.

I use this story to anchor my belief that you should let your potential bedmates talk through their ableism with you before the sexual activity takes place. While I don't think that it's a disabled person's obligation to educate anyone (particularly in a vulnerable moment like sex), I do feel that the opportunity to change a person's worldview on disability is a beautiful thing, and I long for the chance to do that with someone. Talking through the ableism with a partner is a valuable exercise for a few reasons: 1) As the disabled person, you may realize that their ableism isn't meant to hurt you at all; they may just be confused, and have a lack of knowledge, understanding and education on certain aspects of sex and disability, and *you* get to provide that to them. That's hot as fuck. 2) Talking about their ableism with you gives them a safe space to actually have that conversation. I think that ableism persists because people with ableist feelings aren't given places to lay them out—to truly understand where they stem from, and how they have manifested in their lives. Instead, they are told that it isn't appropriate or it isn't nice, or they are ridiculed for having an ableist assumption—trust me when I tell you, I have definitely chimed in with the chorus of people doing the ridiculing, and it isn't helpful. As a result of this inability to ask questions, people have all these misguided half-truths about disability that never get resolved. Talking it out helps them to be honest and, in my opinion, bolsters intimacy and honesty. Try it out with a partner yourself, but remember, it's okay to let them know what your boundaries are around this, as they will be a little different for everyone.

3. Discuss your accessibility needs in the bedroom
This one is one of the hardest things I have ever had to tell someone. In our sex-obsessed culture—one that is unapologetically consumed by able-bodiedness—we have come to

understand that sex is an independent act, and that if you can't be independent you can't truly have sex. There is absolutely no room for discussions of accessibility, disability, support or care at all. It is my belief that we don't talk about these things because we mistakenly believe that it will somehow detract from the passion that we are supposed to engage in. I hate to admit that I too have fallen victim to this, and so for a long time I didn't discuss any of my needs. I can remember so many times where I would chat with a potential player and simply tell them, "I am in a wheelchair. Is that okay?" thinking that this was enough information for them to understand what was required of them. In my youthful attempts to remain cool and crippled, I never gave them any instruction on how to actually get me out of my wheelchair—whoops.

Discussing your accessibility needs in the bedroom is fucking terrifying—there's no other way I can put it. All of your vulnerability is laid bare in that moment, and at any second a partner could realize that your needs are way too much for them to deal with and bolt out of the room, which is horribly ableist and happens all too often. It has happened to me at least six times. Despite all that, if you discuss your accessibility in the bedroom with a partner, you actually begin to get to know each other more deeply in the bedroom than you may have expected to. By sharing that you have a special lift to go from your mobility aid to the bed, and that you'll need help with that, you crack open the facade of sexuality and ability that we all hold far too close. It isn't a fantasy anymore; it is all too real, and with it comes a rush better than the sex you're about to have: being vulnerable. Being vulnerable is one of my favorite parts about sex and disability, and sharing our needs with a partner builds a trust unlike any other.

I remember once I was in my lift above my bed being transferred, and without thinking my sex worker cradled my head so that I would be more comfortable. As I rested my head in his hand, and let him position me, I felt incredibly scared. Right there, he was seeing that I was different from everyone else. As I was being hoisted above my bed in a big machine, there was no hiding my reality of disability anymore. In my head, I imagined that I was being transported as though I was some alien creature with spastic tentacles. Everything inside me wanted to scream and hide. All I could think was, "Oh my god, I am fucking severely disabled, and he knows it! Why the fuck would he want me?" After he made sure I was comfy on the bed, he cuddled with me and we just lay in the comfortable discomfort of that moment together. It was one of the most beautiful moments of intimacy I have shared with someone, and it all happened because I said, "I need help to get into bed."

I remember another moment where I told a guy I was hooking up with that it was hard for me to give him head in my wheelchair because I couldn't reach him. Without thinking, he stood up on a chair and said, "Is that better now?" It was so quick, and a simple fix to a big anxiety that I had. In a split second, he made it so that I could pleasure him, and I was so happy in that moment because the sex was finally reciprocal.

4. Hire a sex worker or bodyworker

One of the best things I have done to enhance my sex life as a severely disabled person has been to work with and build relationships with sex workers to have my needs met. Until seven or eight years ago, I had the misguided beliefs about sex workers that we all hear. I believed that it was a seedy, danger-ous thing to do. I felt that I shouldn't have to hire someone, because I was good looking enough that I ought to be able to meet someone the "normal way" (whatever the fuck "normal" was anyway), and I didn't have to go this route. I can remember thinking to myself, "I'm not like those poor saps. They're desperate." Funnily enough, in 2015, I was indeed that desperate.

It was coming up to November of that year, and I remember that I was in a completely foul mood for a few months. I was angry because I couldn't self-pleasure, and I hadn't had intimacy in about ten months. No one had touched me other than my attendants, and I was starting to feel it in my heart. So, one night I was scrolling through an escort site, one that I would always find myself coming back to but then would abruptly click away from, convincing myself that there must be a better way to do this, must be a better way to get the gratification that I longed for.

I couldn't stop thinking about this site (if I'm completely honest, I couldn't stop thinking about the hot guys on the site, each of them offering something slightly different from the last). I said "fuck it" and hopped on the site. One profile caught my eye—he was scruffy, muscular and had the most beautiful silvery blue eyes I'd ever seen. After scrolling through his enticing photos, I looked at his rate card: $300 an hour. Looking at my wallet, I knew that while I couldn't afford it, I'd figure something out to make it work. I reached out and asked him if he had ever been with a disabled client before. He said, "No, I haven't" and I got excited. I realized then that since he had never been with a disabled client before, he might not have any ableism towards the idea either. I told him what I was looking for, paid the money and we set a date.

For days before our meeting, I wracked my brain about whether or not I made the right decision. I could have used that money for anything else. Buying groceries to feed myself, for one. I was also terrified that he'd see my disability and run away from me. He didn't. While he was nervous about hurting me and unsure about my needs as a disabled person, we made it work and have been working together the last seven years. Working with a sex worker has given me the confidence to look at my sexuality differently. He has helped me feel sexy and know that I have sexual value. I think that if you have the means to hire someone, you should look into it. One of the things that I really enjoy is knowing when he's coming over, because I can finally unleash my sexual energy. Let me offer a few crip tips on how to hire a sex worker when you have a disability.

BE UPFRONT ABOUT YOUR DISABILITY

I know that some part of sex work is the fantasy you're creating with them. In order to make the fantasy work, they need to know exactly what they're working with. So, if you need help in and out of your mobility aid, tell them. Nobody wants a surprise wheelchair they weren't really expecting, and if you're honest, you'll get better bang for your buck, I promise.

PAY THEM UPFRONT AND DON'T ASK FOR DISCOUNTS

For many disabled folks, money can be tight. So, if you plan on hiring someone, be sure you have the funds to do so, before you see them. I was once in a situation where a new worker I was seeing stole some money from me, so just be cautious. It may be wise to pay them after the session. Another important thing is not to ask for discounts. I understand the temptation for a lot of us who don't have a lot of money and are craving intimacy, but it is their job.

DON'T GET TOO ATTACHED

This one was hard for me. Because I am disabled, and don't often get touched intimately, I have learned that I am a lover and I like mushy, consistent shows of affection. I'm basically perpetually 17 in that regard. I'll watch those silly rom-coms over and over and imagine myself as the Meg Ryan protagonist.

So, when I first started seeing my worker friend, I bombarded him constantly and we had to work on boundary setting. I was so excited because I had never had someone come back and want to see me again, so I put a ton of pressure on him to fulfill all these things for me, which was really unfair. So, I would say, enjoy your time with the worker and if you build a rapport or a friendship, that's awesome. But, no matter how tempting it may be when you feel that rush of endorphins and connection the first time, remember that they are working with you. Keeping that in the back of your mind may alleviate any pulling on the heartstrings that may occur.

I hope these tips help a little. Go forth and own your sexual journey, and if that means coming (or cumming) to a professional, do what works for you. Show those awesome sex workers that disabled people are hot!

5. Turn your mobility aid into one big sex toy— no, really!

I remember one time I was in my power wheelchair and my sex worker gave me a surprise blowjob in my chair. He anchored himself on my armrest, kissed me passionately, lowered himself to my crotch and went to town. It was one of the most sensual things I have ever done because it was using something I was terrified of (my wheelchair) and turning it into a tool for pleasure. Here we were in the middle of my room, he on his knees and me moaning in ecstasy in my wheelchair—this thing that gives me freedom in so many ways, but restricts me in so many others. In this medical thing, I could get off, and that has been so freeing in and of itself.

I hold this moment close in my sexual journey because we have been conditioned to see our mobility aids as these sterile, detached devices that only have one purpose. If you get the opportunity to use your mobility aid as a sexual pleasure aid, do it. Maybe your walker could stabilize you for doggy style, or your wheelchair could be the perfect cushion for someone to sit on. The possibilities are really endless, and incorporating your mobility aids may really help remove some of the internalized ableism we all experience when we are trying to be sexual beings.

Have I really had the best sex ever as a disabled person?

What I have learned being a severely disabled person is that the "best sex" really is a myth. You can have all the fantasies and expectations about what a sexual encounter is meant to be, and you will still run into issues of external ableism, internalized ableism, fear, adaptation and so on. Because of my own internalized ableism (it's a daily struggle), I'll probably never think that I have had the best sex ever, but I hope that these suggestions can act as a guide for you to start loving your disabled sex.

CHAPTER 4

No Ramps in Hollywood

Making Queer Spaces Accessible (No, Really!)

remember being invited to this big queer party in Hollywood. My podcast, *Disability After Dark*, had been nominated in 2020 for Best Queer Podcast at an awards show put on by a prominent queer magazine. I was so excited to learn of this—that the little show I created in my bedroom had gained enough recognition to bring me to Hollywood. What?! I immediately clicked on my phone and started looking up flights to go. I called my mom, who is one of my best friends and often acts as my attendant care person when I travel for things like this. She was excited too, so we booked a flight and got ourselves ready for a few days of glitz and glamor together in La La Land.

After taking a five-hour flight to get to Los Angeles, we were pleasantly surprised to find that for once, my power wheelchair was not damaged. For those of you who may not be regular wheelchair users, allow me to explain why finding my wheelchair in one piece was something to be elated by. I have been flying on airplanes with my power chair since I was eight years old, and almost every time I flew, my wheelchair came off the plane damaged or unusable. Sometimes, I couldn't drive the chair because the guys handling it had unplugged something, or it was so mangled when I received it that I would have to spend a day in the hotel room waiting for a repair man to come and look at it, only to tell me that they didn't have the part. Having your wheelchair damaged has become a part of traveling, and it is something that in this day and age speaks to the ableism that we all still have to work on.

I could ramble on and on about this, but for now, I'll just say that we were so happy to find the wheelchair in working order. From here, we hit the Hollywood Walk of Fame with a shower commode and my mom in tow as we looked for our hotel (we had a friend get us a room at the swanky Roosevelt Hotel, the place where Marilyn Monroe lived for a while, and countless celebs have stayed). We had to deal with accessibility needs the whole way through, but the night of the big party finally arrived.

I was so nervous. I had never been to a big party like this before. My mom and I dashed around our hotel room, finding the right combination of clothes to wear. My mom was the perfect person to help me with this—she was an esthetician by trade, so she knew how to make me look just right to shine at a party. I chose a bright blue shirt and a pink boa to add a little bit of flare, and off we went. You might think because we were in Los Angeles, the entertainment capital of the world, that it would be easy for us to find accessible transit to the venue, right? Well, you'd be wrong on that one. We called a number of cab companies, each of them telling us that they either would be there in three to four hours or they had no cabs that could take a power wheelchair. So, we decided to walk there. Luckily, the venue was only a few blocks away from our hotel. The closer and closer that we got to the building, the more nervous I found myself. I could see people heading that way, all of them dressed fabulously in one way or another.

When we finally walked into the bar, it was done up to look really nice. There were big screens on either side of the room, and every now and then my podcast logo would flash up on the screen. I remember trying not to be too excited and to remain cool in that moment (ha! Whatever cool means anyway), but I definitely didn't. As I scanned the room, I saw queer influencers everywhere, talking and laughing, basking in the glow of their shared identity, safe in the knowledge that they could access their queerness whenever they wanted to. One of the things I didn't see, though, was another wheelchair user in the room. I was it. On realizing this, I had a confluence of emotions to contend with. I was proud to be representing a community of queer, disabled wheelchair users; it was so pivotal and important that I was in the room at all. I was sending a message to all the other queers in the room that I deserved to be there taking up space with them—and I wouldn't trade that feeling for anything at all. They did a little red carpet thing for all of us, and I remember watching my wheels go across the carpet and smiling, thinking about just how many big queer spaces I had felt excluded from, as if I didn't matter at all. And, here I was on a fucking red carpet in my power chair in Hollywood. For just a moment, in that moment, I felt iconic. I was having pictures taken and giving interviews, all of this solidifying my commitment to being queer and disabled in this room full of people who probably hadn't given disability a thought.

My feelings of elation quickly dissipated. I was there being nominated for an award, remember, so there was a big stage that was meant to draw everyone's attention. I peeled my eyes away from a really cute influencer in my eyeline, and as they walked away, I knew that I wasn't going to win the award that night. Unfortunately, my disability doesn't come with a side of all-knowing or anything, but as I looked past the cutie, I saw that the stage had no ramp attached to it. My heart sank. Not only was this a clear indication that I wasn't taking home a stat-uette (there were no statuettes, that was just used to paint you a picture), but it was also a signal to me that the organizers hadn't truly considered my needs while being there. I won't pretend that didn't sting somewhat, so Mom and I listened to some of the speeches and left early to go and eat burgers on Hollywood Boulevard and laugh at the absurdity and inaccessibility of it all. It was a good night, no matter what, and something that I will never forget.

I started the chapter using that story as my anchor, because I want to explore how we make queer spaces actually accessible for disabled folks. It starts with making sure that there are ramps, interpreters and accessible washrooms at award shows and queer parties, but I believe it has to go a lot deeper than that. Let me explain using another example.

There was a big queer party one night in the middle of summer a few years back. It was right in the heart of the de-liciously debauched queerness that happens every Friday and Saturday night at downtown spots. You know, shirtless queer boys dancing and flirting—that whole vibe. I had heard that one of my favorite porn stars was going to be there dancing the night away. I was determined to go and unleash myself at this party. I thought, "Here is my chance to be seen." I remember that it took me hours of planning and rearranging my life to be there. I had to book two accessible wheelchair buses, each one needing to be timed to the minute so that I would get there okay. I spent a day and a half on hold getting the buses figured out, not to mention the fact that I had to coordinate my drinking and water intake, so that when I left home, I wouldn't be stranded somewhere between the club and home, all alone and needing to pee.

Anyone who has had to do "pee math" knows exactly what I am talking about. For those of you reading who may not know about this particular equation, allow me to expand on it for you. Pee math is an equation that disabled people employ before we leave the accessibility of our homes and go anywhere. We consider how much we can drink before we'll need to pee again; we consider how long we'll be gone and whether or not it's worth hydrating at all, especially if the washrooms we'll encounter in the wild aren't accessible to us. Pee math takes up so much of our time as disabled folks, and I certainly haven't got it down to a science, but I hope that you understand a little better now.

All of this planning and coordination felt like a full-time job on its own. But, needless to say, I had worked it all out and I was going. I had the nervous butterflies, hoping and praying that it would be a good time. Okay, if I'm honest with you all, I hoped that the porn star would see me at this party and want to take me home or something.

The night finally came. The party didn't start until 10pm, but I had to leave my house at 7pm to get on the two accessible transit buses just to be there on time. I did all of this, making sure not to drink too much as we got closer to the bar. As all the guys filed in, sweaty, shirtless and full of potential, I came in behind them in my wheelchair. I remember that as I rolled around the venue in my power wheelchair, while I found it very physically accessible for me to be in the space, there was now another level of access that I had to consider: emotional accessibility.

Every time that I saw a group of guys that I wanted to talk with, I wheeled over in my chair, and I saw their faces change— almost immediately. They went from a jovial, lively, happy conversation to seeing me and being frozen in fear. It was as if they had seen an alien with three heads approach them. Those kind of guys didn't know what to do at all, so they just stared and closed ranks around themselves. There were also the guys who looked at me as if I didn't dare belong, and that somehow my whole presence was ruining their night. They had certainly perfected the "mean gay" trope, and every time I tried to intro- duce myself to one of them, I was met with smiles full of pity and annoyance. I was reminded in that moment that these guys I was wanting to connect with were not emotionally accessible to me, and ever since then I have wondered how to change that. How to make queer, non-disabled community members get in touch with that emotional accessibility so that they can start to see queer disabled people as viable, vital community members. Let's look at some ways we can do that, and then explore more ways to make queer spaces accessible together!

We need conversations about disability at the queer club

When I give talks about queerness, sexuality and disability, I am usually doing so in a university lecture hall. I love doing it this way, because I know that I am influencing the next gener- ation of queer folks to think about the intersection of disability within the rainbow. I'm also very aware of the fact that these conversations need to be happening outside academia. These conversations can feel safest in the academic bubble, but sometimes it can feel as if the ableism we're talking about lives only in a hypothetical space, and that's a big problem. These conversations need to be taking place where queerness goes to party. We need to have these conversations at the club. It is my dream to rent out a big, kinky leather bar somewhere and use that space to talk about disability. Why, you may ask? Because it will force queer people to look at and confront disability in the spaces that they actually frequent—the spaces where they have cultivated queer community themselves. Every time I picture this happening in my head, I can't help but imagine a big, burly muscle daddy in his leathers being asked to talk about and confront his own ableism. In my head, I also picture a cute go-go dancer sitting down and thinking about the ways that, in the same spaces where he dances his weekends away, he may have perpetuated ableism. We see a lot of couplings, crazy parties and other things that start with c at these clubs, but rarely do we see these conversations, and it's time for that to change.

Gently get queer non-disabled men to talk about ableism

One of the ways that I think we need to foster that emotional accessibility among queer non-disabled men is getting them to talk about their ableism. Now, when I say this, I don't mean calling someone out on their ableist behaviors. Rather, I see this as an opportunity for these queer men to speak their truth around disability, no matter what that looks like. Maybe disability scares the absolute fuck out of some of these guys, even if they are interested in a disabled person. Maybe they've had an experience around disability in their lives that transformed how they thought about disabled people, and they've never been given a chance to express that because they were afraid they might be saying something offensive. Queer non-disabled folks need the opportunity to be honest about ableism, without fear that the honesty will get them shut down.

I know you might be reading this section thinking, "But, Andrew, there's just SO MUCH ableism, we gotta call it out." I get that, trust me, I do. Calling someone on their stuff, especially ableism, feels fucking good. I worry, though, that it shuts down conversation altogether, and thus ends an opportunity for growth and change. If non-disabled queers were given a chance to say, "I saw this disabled guy last week at Starbucks and I was going to approach him, but, like, what if he needed me? I was scared shitless" and share these feelings in an open forum, maybe we'd start moving past the fear that is so prevalent among queer non-disabled people. Just a thought.

Now I'd like to shift the conversation a little bit in an effort to explore some things that you as a queer cripple can do to make your time in queer spaces a little bit easier.

Visit the space before the event

I know just how physically inaccessible queer spaces can be. When sitting in a 250lb power chair that you can often only just squeeze into a corner of a club, you often find that you are in the way of someone. Unfortunately, that is just the reality. If you are able to physically get into the club with your mobility aid, I recommend asking the club owner or the cute barback if you can visit the space before a big night. This is a great option so that you can see the layout of the club and identify the spots where you might not be as visible if you don't want to be.

I am speaking about this as a wheelchair user, but I also want to make sure that my other crip queens who use other devices like walkers, canes or guide dogs think about this too. Going to the space beforehand will give you the opportunity to see if your guide dog is comfy in the space, if your walker will fit, and if your attendant/caregiver can come too—because every queer cripple deserves a night out, and they certainly don't need the anxiety and worry of spatial logistics when all they want is someone all up in their space.

Grab a gimp to go bag

One of the things that I have learned going to queer events is just how bad the washrooms are in those spaces—I kid you not, some of them are literally closets. I have come out of the queer closet and the disability closet time and time and time again, and I don't want to go back in the closet to pee. No thank you!

I have discovered that having a to-go bag with all my supplies at the ready is one of the ways that I can ensure bathroom accessibility anywhere while at a queer event, and it makes things so much easier. That way, if the cutie you've been eyeing all night finally gets over his fear around your disability and decides to take you home, you have all that you'll need. In my bag, I usually have catheters to pee, condoms to play, baby wipes, gauze, water and snacks—you know, the essentials.

Portable ramps

Because queer spaces tend to be in tiny bars that have been closed and re-opened a hundred times over, it is not uncommon, in my experience, to encounter one or two tiny steps to get into these places. I remember once I was doing a sexy photo shoot at one of the sex clubs in Toronto. This was at the start of my career of talking about sex and disability, and an acquaintance of mine had suggested that we go to a bathhouse and do a disability photo shoot, exploring queerness and disability in all its forms. I met him down there on a Friday evening (having to take two paratransit buses again, I left my house at 4pm, wearing a sex harness underneath my clothes), ready and willing to take some hot shots. When we pulled up to the entrance we realized there was but a single, solitary slab of cement that made it difficult for my power wheelchair to get over. I remember the photographer pulling my wheelchair up the concrete slab and struggling to get me inside.

I'm sure that we huffed and puffed for about 30 minutes, wheels spinning, people offering to help, me sitting in my wheelchair annoyed that this is what I had to do just to gain entry here. I stayed as calm as possible, but I remember having trouble relaxing into my "hot disabled guy pose" because of how much trouble I had getting into the space at all. You may think it was just a slab of concrete, but it sent a pretty loud message that queers who use mobility aids were not welcome at all.

This memory I've shared is just one reason why, if you are a queer wheelchair user, you may also want to invest in a portable ramp for yourself when entering a queer club. It won't work every single time at every single venue, but if the club has one big slab of concrete at the entrance, it might create a doable option.

Hold a fundraiser for accessibility in queer spaces

I know you're probably thinking to yourself, "But, Andrew, why do I have to prepare these things for myself? Shouldn't the predominantly white, cis, able-bodied club owners take some responsibility here, too? Shouldn't they do what they can to offer me access?" Yes, they should, but they usually need incentive. They need some kind of push to make it accessible.

I believe that just as we have drag brunches and big, elaborate parties for HIV and AIDS research—and as vital as those events are—accessibility is equally important. Why can't we call on personalities like Trixie Mattel and Bob the Drag Queen to host an extravagant gala for accessibility in every major club in every major city? I picture go-go dancers and drag performers mingling with people throughout the night and for every $50,000 donated, a different club gets renovated. And, let's face it, there's money in the gay community. One of the most prominent gays out there is Anderson Cooper, who in 2024, was reportedly worth $50 million. You're telling me we couldn't get Anderson Cooper, Billy Porter, Gus Kenworthy and a bunch of other high profile homos to help make lack of accessibility in queer spaces a thing of the past? We could do that, and we should do that, but we don't because that would mean that we'd have to confront the hard facts that most queer men don't want disabled people in their clubs.

The next time you see a push for a queer event raising money for community, call up Gus Kenworthy and—no, no, I'm just kidding—ask them if even 10 percent of the proceeds could go towards making queer clubs accessible. If you are a non-disabled queer person and you happen to be reading this, and you want to know what you can do, planning a party to fund accessibility is a big start. Asking about accessibility at every event you attend is a big start. Helping to make sure that disability justice is on the radar of the club owners is a big start. We have to start somewhere, and not having ramps at an awards show where a disabled person is nominated is just not good enough.

My dream club—what I wish accessibility in queer spaces actually looked like

As a disabled person in a power wheelchair who is unable to fully access queer spaces, I often imagine what a fully accessible queer disabled club would look like. In my mind's eye, I can picture it to a tee. I can see the room crammed full of people, disabled and non-disabled alike, each of them there to enjoy a booming Saturday drag show, or a Sunday funday underwear party. I want to share with you, dear reader, what my accessible club looks like. Come on in, won't you?

For the entry way, I envision big ramps that light up as you walk or wheel down them (because disabled queers deserve to make a fucking entrance). I imagine that these ramps will be flat, not steep in any way. Unlike our modern idea of accessibility, the entry way to this bar will be at the front of the building, and when you enter, the doors will open automatically, no buttons required at all.

When you enter the club, you will be immediately met by an attendant who will help you take off your outside clothes and adorn whatever attire makes you feel the most sexy. They will be there to help you with any personal care needs throughout the evening, from using the washroom to prepping for playtime with the cutie across the bar. So often, queer disabled people have to navigate their intersectionality of queerness and disability while alone in these spaces, thus making asking for help or support impossible or embarrassing. My dream club will change all of that.

The club will never use strobe lights, scents or anything else that might cause sensory overload because we understand that this club isn't just for the wheelchair-using queer cripple, it is to be an experience that all can enjoy. To that end, the club has an area for guide dogs, which includes water bowls and a rest area. I have never seen a service dog in a queer club, and that definitely needs to change.

As you look around the club, you see that the ceilings are very high. Each ceiling beam has a Hoyer lift and a track fixed to it, so that should clubbers want to get out of their mobility aids and cozy up next to someone, they can do that.

If you need to pee at the club, every washroom is equipped with wide doors for power chairs, braille on all signage for the cute blind folks out there, and every single stall is accessible.

They each have Hoyer lifts, adult changing tables, and adult sex tables in them, because why shouldn't disabled folks get to experience hot bathroom sex in the accessible stalls? Everyone else seems to.

Every night would be #DisabledPeopleAreHot night, and everyone is welcome. From walker users, to wheelchair users, to guide dog owners, to those with disabilities we cannot see, no one is excluded.

All of these things seem like big asks right now, but really they aren't.

CHAPTER 5

The Importance of Representation (and That Time This Cripple Made a Porno!)

I remember hearing the ding on my phone one morning indicating that a text had come through. It was probably just an attendant care worker letting me know they'd be running a little bit later than they usually were to wake me up, or it was a scam text waiting for me to input my details so they could steal all my money. My phone beeped again, waiting for me to answer. As my eyes adjusted and I read the text, I couldn't quite comprehend what I'd just read. No way. This isn't real. As I reread the text over and over, a grin crept across my face that I couldn't contain any longer. The text I received was from my friend, a gay porn producer who I had got to know a little bit over the years.

In the little gray bubble on my iPhone, I saw that he was asking me to be in an adult film that he wanted to launch on his website, dedicated to gay male erotica and pleasure. I was very excited by this prospect. I had been talking about the need to see disabled bodies in gay porn for years now, but talking was all that I'd had the courage to do. Deep down inside I had way more feelings than I let to the surface, and I want to share some now. I wanted there to be disabled bodies in gay porn, but my internalized ableism and shame around my own disabled body made the idea of that person being me impossible. The devil on my shoulder whispering all the dark thoughts in my ear was telling me that my disabled body was gross, that no one wanted to see my crooked spine on camera, and that since I can't even thrust into another guy, what good was I in the bedroom.

As I tried to figure out what I was even going to type in response, while simultaneously quieting the self-doubting devil, who at this point was screaming show-tune-level melodies of fear in my ear, I lifted up my phone and began typing. "Sure, I'd love to," I typed against my better judgment. Even though I was scared fucking shitless about the idea of actually doing something like this, I knew that it was bigger than just me. I knew that putting out a video of a severely disabled person in a porn film would do so much for disabled people's sexual representation, especially in the queer community—a place where our bodies were not seen or heard from at all.

I grabbed my phone again and quickly jotted out a text message to my sex worker. He was the only one I really trusted in this regard, and he knew how to make me feel safe and sexy all at the same time. I let him know of the plans, and asked if he would do it with me. He said yes. This. Was. Happening. There was no turning back now, and that truth scared me more than I realized. Once it was all set up, for days I doubted myself. I kept thinking that I would never live up to the ideal gay porn star. I wouldn't do well enough, I couldn't do well enough; my disabled body simply wasn't worth enough for something like this. Yeah, those internalized ableism tapes got replayed a whole lot as the project drew closer.

About two weeks later, in the middle of October, I was sitting in my living room with my favorite sex worker and we were talking about how we wanted to block the scene we were about to film. To be honest, this was one of my favorite parts of the whole thing; talking about how my disability and all that entails would be shown in the scene. I had made abundantly clear that I wanted my wheelchair and my Hoyer lift to be prominently displayed in the scene. I felt it was crucial to show the reality of queer disabled sex, no matter what that looked like to an outside audience. So much of disability in media representation glosses over the truth of it all; the nitty gritty bits tend to be expunged so that the audience is left with a pristine version of disability, one that leaves them inspired to see the world a little bit brighter. One that's not even talking about sexuality and disability at all. Seeing sexuality and disability represented on screen is still a rarity, and if it is done we usually see it from the lens of an able-bodied, non-disabled person who is the partner of the disabled person, and we usually only see how the non-disabled partner copes with the burden of their disabled partner's body. All that to say, I knew that showing a disabled person being sexualized in their wheelchair was a big fucking swing, and I was ready for it.

There is also a scene showing me in my sling, being transferred to my bed. I fucking adored this scene, because no one ever knows how disabled people have sex, or how they get into bed or what that looks like, and this would show them unequivocally what goes into bedding someone like me. I remember feeling my nerves melt away as my sex worker, Ben, guided me through how to have sex on camera. He made me feel so safe and secure in what we were doing, that eventually I didn't even notice the camera as it zoomed up close and personal on my disabled body. My spastic limbs full on with desire and cerebral palsy as they grabbed, pawed and clutched onto every second of that experience. At one point, Ben hoisted himself up on my lift motor so that I could give him pleasure, and I loved seeing my medical device being used as an object of pleasure. That was a game changer. Okay, it was also just fucking hot, but it helped to put disability on the sexual map in a way that I don't really believe that anyone had considered before.

After the scene was done, I remember that he and I lay there, my head on his chest, me panting from the very real experience we shared together, and I couldn't stop smiling from ear to ear. There I was in a puddle of my own palsied pleasure, having made a film showing me having actual disabled sex. How powerful, how important, and how long overdue. Right? I haven't made any adult films since that one (if any studios are interested, I am available, LOL) but I am so proud of what we made. A few months after its release, I was asked by a few sex educators if they could use the video so that they could educate up and coming educators on sexuality and disability. I am so honored by that because knowing that they will use my video to change sexual attitudes of the next generations—wow.

I share that story as a kicking-off point to this chapter because I want to talk about the kinds of queer cripple representation that I want to see. In the last chapter, we imagined what the dream accessible club might look like. In this chapter, let's imagine the kinds of TV shows, movies and magazines where that club might show up. Let's talk about the kind of queer cripple representation that is long overdue, and the positive impact that having queer disabled representation can have on everything.

The disabled queer romantic comedy

Every time I watch a queer rom-com or anything like that on Netflix, I always imagine what it might be like if one or both of the characters had a disability. One of the scenarios that I think would make for a fantastic queer disabled romantic comedy is having the main characters wait for a paratransit bus every day that is always late or that never shows up at all, and during that time they fall in love with one another. Trust me when I tell you, this is a very common thing that happens in disability circles, but it is very rarely understood by someone who doesn't use those services, so putting that into a rom-com sends an important message of inclusion to queer disabled people.

I would also love to see representation that includes a disabled queer character grappling with their own internalized ableism. So much of queer disabled romance includes the self-doubt of being disabled. You ask yourself questions like, "Am I good enough?" or, "Does my disability get in the way?" or, "Do I hold sexual value as a disabled person?" If I'm honest, I have yet to see a fully fleshed out disabled character who is talking about these realities of the queer cripple experience—and it is about freaking time, in my opinion, that we have characters who are showing audiences these truths that we deal with every day.

Another thing that I would love to see in a queer disabled rom-com, or any movie about queer disabled love, is for the disabled character to love themselves enough to call out the ableism they experience trying to access a relationship. In almost all disability representation that I have seen, nobody uses the word ableism, and I think if queer audiences especially saw that word being used in their media, it may give them a jumping off point to recognize moments in the queer experience where they have been ableist, and I think that is so important.

The queer disabled drama

One of my most favorite pieces of media about queer sexuality and identity was Andrew Haigh's 2011 film *The Weekend*. It was such a simple piece about a queer one night stand that develops into something more. I would love to see a film like that dealing with the realities of disability. Imagine that a hookup comes to my door, walks into my home and sees all my disability equipment, and then realizes just how disabled I actually am. How would that play out onscreen? I think it would be so rich and vibrant to watch both characters navigate their own ableism as they explore sexuality and disability together. In all my time talking about sex and disability, people continually remind me that my body scares them—the reality of my needs terrifies them. Seeing this played out in a sexy, dark, funny, brooding queer crip scenario would be groundbreaking. I feel as if it would give queer non-disabled viewers avenues with which to examine their own discomfort around sex and disability in a way that is personal and accessible to them. Plus, it would have a few hot make-out and bedding scenes using disability equipment, and that is the true representation that I feel we are missing.

The queer disabled horror film

Over the last couple years, it seems there has been a big push towards queer horror in cinema. Every few queer film festivals will have a campy horror film with laughs, lots of drag and a lot of sexual tension; and then there is one that always leaves the audience feeling unsettled... This is the story that makes queerness the dangerous thing in the room; the one that turns the comfortable, relatable queer person into the thing to be feared. Those are always my favorite ones, if I'm honest. I feel it would be groundbreaking to have a horror movie called *Queer Cripple*. Imagine a movie following a severely disabled queer as they attempt to enter a club, and when they can't, the audience realizes that the disabled person isn't the villain, ableism is. There is such a long history of disabled people being misread as the villain: the vampire, the deranged mental patient, the mangled monster...this list could go on and on. If we made ableism the villain it could do so much for queer cinema. Allow me, if you will, dear reader, to pitch an idea I had:

Andy and Mark are making out in the dark room of the only accessible club in town. The room is thick with desire; Mark is climbing all over Andy, unbuttoning his seat belt, climbing over his power wheelchair so that he can devour even more of him. Mark has never been with a disabled guy before, but this is so hot!

Andy can't believe this is happening to him. Finally! A non-disabled

87

guy wants him. It feels like a dream. Every touch, every caress more vibrant, more electrically charged than the one before it. Andy keeps checking in, waiting for the moment Mark will realize he's disabled and bolt for the door. The next thing Andy knows Mark is between his legs, and they're both moaning in the throes of ecstasy. Mark looks up at Andy, and as Andy looks in his eyes, for a split second the warm, inviting eyes have shifted. All of a sudden, Mark's eyes look robotic, sick almost. All of a sudden, Mark adopts a creepy, intense grin. From between Andy's legs he screams, "So, what happened to you?" Andy is stunned as he realizes that the virus of ableism has overtaken his lover. Like a zombie, ableist phrases spew from his mouth. Andy tries to back his chair up, tries to get away as fast as his wheelchair will take him. He must outrun the ableism.

Pretty fucking scary, hey?

The queer disabled reality show—crip up the club

Okay, ever since *Queer Eye for the Straight Guy* came on the queer media scene, I have had an idea percolating in the back of my mind. What if a bunch of queer disabled people, each with different disabilities, went around to prominent queer bars in North America and found ways to make them accessible? Kind of a cross between *Queer Eye* and *Sparking Joy with Marie Kondo*, but instead of joy, we ask if something is accessible? I think this would be an incredible way to showcase how we can make queer spaces accessible, while simultaneously highlighting how different disabilities have different access needs. It could be a weekly series on a big network like NBC, ABC or Netflix (seriously, call me) and I think that seeing these types of accommodations on a regular basis would keep queerness and disability top of mind for so many, when it all too often gets couched in "very special episodes" of shows, if it is considered at all. I mean, can you imagine a show where once a week a queer club is updated to include disabled people, and after every renovation there is a sexy as fuck queer dance party? Sign me up, please.

The crippled drag race

I'll be honest, I'm not big on *Drag Race* myself. I have never found it all that interesting, and I guess that's because so much of drag feels like a ton of able-bodied privilege that I, as a queer cripple, don't have. So many of the queens have abilities to craft looks and personas that I can't access on my own as a disabled person.

So, I'd love to tweak the concept a little bit. Okay, let's be real, I wanna crip it the fuck up! Why can't we have a bunch of disabled drag queens who have to be dressed and made up in their looks by non-disabled participants? I think this would be such a playful critique on the inaccessibility of the drag scene, and highlight just how much of it needs to adapt so that everyone can actually participate. Instead of a catwalk, there could be one big ramp. Instead of lip-sync for your life, crip-sync for your life. There could be an outfit that has to look good when you go out with your service animal, and funny, accessible nods like that to make the idea of disability something drag embraces and learns about!

Queer disabled roundtables

In 2013, I auditioned for a little Canadian TV show called *1 Girl 5 Gays*. It was a late-night roundtable show that aired on MTV Canada and later in the US on Logo, where five prominent Toronto gay men would sit on a circle and be asked increasingly intimate questions by a girl. The show ran for eight seasons (I think), and kind of became a staple of queer media in the mid 2000s. I watched it on occasion, and every time I did I never saw anyone who looked like me; you know, hot, queer, crippled and in a wheelchair. So, one day I emailed the producers and very brazenly let them know that they needed me on the show so there would be fuller representation of all queer experiences. I sent the email off and thought nothing of it, assuming they probably get emails like this all the time, and they wouldn't get back to me.

Two weeks later, as I was hunting for work, an email flashed in my inbox. It was the producers of the show! They wanted me to come in for an interview. I was so excited! I hadn't had any kind of TV experience back then, so I went in completely fresh. I told them that there hadn't been enough queer disabled representation in the media, and I could ensure they were at the forefront of this change. I left full of adrenaline and excitement, but also fear. If they picked me, I would most likely be the only disabled wheelchair user in the room, and that can be a daunting, lonely place to be.

Sure enough, a few months later as I pulled up to the MTV Canada building in downtown Toronto, and was ushered into the green room where the cast was welcomed in, that fear was confirmed. As the cast came in, I didn't see anyone at all who resembled my queer experience. Everyone could choose where they wanted to sit on big comfy couches, and I had to be in the same spot each time I was on. I couldn't sit on the couches, so I parked my wheelchair as close as I could to them, so that I could be included. Funnily enough, it mirrored my experiences of being queer and disabled out in the world. You're there, just not in the same way as everyone else is. Every episode that I was on that season, I made sure to scream about disability; even if we were talking about queering up the club or how to give the best blowjob, I made sure the disability experience was front and center, probably to the annoyance of a few cast members.

I would love to see shows like that—shows that feature all disabled queer folks alongside one non-disabled queer person. Why not *1 Queer 5 Cripples*? Or a roundtable show that helps to answer so many of the questions queer people may hold around the queer disabled experience, such as: "How do you have sex?" "What can we do to be anti-ableist in queer spaces?" "What is the best queer crip date you've had?" I think it would be so valuable, and completely groundbreaking and unheard of in the TV/streaming landscape. It would give queer disabled people another weekly platform to be heard and seen by the queer community at large, and that is still something, as I write this, that is a rarity.

Queer magazine covers

Back at the start of my career advocating for queer cripple inclusion, I wanted to get out there and show myself in whatever way I could. One of the pieces of media that I devoured as a queer person was the magazine cover. On queer magazine covers, especially the ones dedicated to queer men, we are used to seeing white, able-bodied men, who have eight packs and ten packs galore, and I ate that type of media up. I also longed to be a part of that kind of media, because I wanted to show off and I wanted to be seen as desirable in my own right as a severely disabled person.

I remember being contacted by *The Gay Times UK* and being asked to write a story about my sex life and how great it was to have disabled sex. I wrote the story using way too many sexual innuendos about touching my big joystick, and after I sent it in, they asked me if I could include any photos of myself in it. Initially, I sent them some crappy screenshots of myself from the 2010s, but they wanted a professional photographer to do it for me, which they would pay for.

So, there I was a few weeks later trying to pose in front of the camera in my power wheelchair. I was in my apartment, with all of these big lights on me, in a black tank top to accentuate my muscles. I was trying so hard to emulate my six packed, non-disabled counterparts, that I almost fell out of my wheelchair. As we were taking the photos, I realized about halfway through that I would never be able to copy what other queer folks had done. No matter what I did to copy the queer poses that I see all other white, abled cis men doing, I felt defeated. It took me forever to get comfy in my disabled skin for that shoot, and I believe that is, in part, because we never see severely disabled people like me on the cover of any queer media at all.

Perhaps if we saw disabled people more regularly on the cover of *The Advocate* or *Out Magazine* or the hundreds of other magazines that live and die yearly, our views on disabled queerness might start to shift. So many of the magazine covers for gay/queer men reinforce the idea that in order for you to be queer you have to look healthy and normative. Wouldn't it be groundbreaking to have a sexy, sick and seated person as part of the magazine, too? It would force gay and queer men to re-confront their own mortality, and their own ableism that is wrapped within that. Having a severely disabled or sick person on the cover of a queer publication would also help queer people living with body issues, whatever those may be, to finally see a version of themselves reflected back to them. And, isn't that more important than what Gus Kenworthy had for breakfast? I think so.

Queer disabled pop songs

As it stands right now, if we look at the musical landscape we have so many songs about love/breakups and relationships. Every time I listen to one of these songs on my Spotify playlist (usually at 2am when I can't sleep), about breaking up, like so many of us, I put myself in that situation. I imagine that some dude has said an ableist thing to me, and I am singing about why he would do that. In all of the songs Taylor Swift puts out (I'm a crippled Swiftie, rest assured), I'm fairly certain she uses the word love eight million times. You know what word we never explore in love songs? Ableism. Can you imagine if there were ballads about the ableism a disabled person experienced trying to date? Pop jams about ableism in the bedroom? Gimpy glam rock? If we had music about ableism in popular culture, our understanding of ableism would grow exponentially.

Let me share an example of what I mean. Sometimes, when I listen to songs, I post the lyrics in an Instagram post, but I change some of the words to depict disability. One of my favorite queer albums is *So Jealous* by Canadian pop superstars Tegan and Sara. I have seen them in concert three times and can recite every lyric. This album is the one that I put on when I want to get over a boy or the ableism I have experienced as a queer cripple. It is a salve that I come back to over and over again because it represents my queer longing and rage so very well. Since I can't use their actual lyrics here, I am going to create lyrics around the ableism that I experience in the style of a Tegan and Sara hit... So, here we go.

I wish you could see me/in my wheelchair/with all the love I have for you

I wish you could see me/sitting there in my wheelchair waiting for you to see all of me too

Sometimes I wish you could be me/in my wheelchair so I know that you might feel all of it too/oooh, ooh, oooh

Here's another potential banger in the same style:

Does my disability scare you? I know it does/even though you say it's fine/I know it's anything but/yeah yeah yeah

Okay, okay, I know it isn't an exact science, and I know that I am definitely not a singer-songwriter by any means (LOL), but there is a whole lot of potential to put queer disability themes in popular culture through music. We have earworms about so much, and a bop about the inaccessibility of disabled desire is just waiting to be written. Also, Tegan and Sara, wanna co-write a bop together?

What would media like this have done for my queer crippled self?

If I had seen media like this when I was coming out as a queer disabled person at 16, or if I had seen representation like this when I came out as a severely disabled queer person last week, the impact would have been monumental. I may have been more confident in who I was; had I seen gay and queer porn with a spastic body like mine in it, I may have been able to feel valued in the bedroom with a non-disabled lover. If a character with my needs fell in love on the big screen in a romantic comedy, maybe I wouldn't have spent half my life trying to downplay my disability in an attempt to have non-disabled queer people accept me. If I had songs that represented the pain of ableist rejection to play in my ears, maybe it wouldn't hurt as bad. Who knows? Maybe seeing media like this would allow me to feel desirable to others, and enjoy that experience instead of constantly considering whether or not my disability is being fetishized.

Media like this would have helped me immensely, but most importantly, I think that by even putting these suggestions on paper somewhere, it can help the next generation create something that is queer, crippled and revolutionary. I hope for you, dear reader, these ideas have got your wheels and gears turning and reminded you that queer disabled people should be everywhere: on your playlists, in your top five fave film characters, on your reality show guilty pleasures. These possible shows, songs, movies and magazines should be saturating our media landscape and filling it with proverbial ramps, elevators and buttons. We should be sick of disabled pop star drama. These media depictions should be the ones that the queer crippled 16-year-olds of today watch with the volume down low, under the covers in the safety of their adjustable beds, giving them permission to be queer. Until then, a cripple can dream, right?

CHAPTER 6

Caring for the Queer Cripple

How Do You Start a Conversation About
Needing Help to Have Sex?

One morning, one of my attendant care workers woke
me up. He had been working in the program I live
in for disabled people for about a year at that point.
Sidebar: The kind of care I receive is known as "supportive
housing," which means that while you live in the apartment
on your own, you are connected with staff who work for an
agency. They are assigned to see you for a certain number of
hours a day (never, ever enough by the way) to help you with
activities of daily living such as showering, eating and using the
bathroom. I have had this kind of care since the age of 16 years
old, so I am fairly adept at managing my needs. Anyway, this
worker and I were fairly comfortable with each other. He was
very, very friendly, and he always was kind to me (his kindness
is important, because a lot of disabled people experience abuse
at the hands of carers).

Anyway, let's call him Peter. About three times a week, Peter
would wake me up, help me shower and get started with my day.
He was funny, with a big laugh that bounced off my apartment

walls with a jubilant echo. His smile was kind, and you could tell that he wanted to make the day for the disabled people in his charge the best it could be. Every morning that I had him, he would saunter in my apartment adorned in a fancy dress shirt, $300 shoes and his priceless smile. He would help me transfer to my commode chair and then wheel me into the bathroom and place me squarely in front of my bathroom mirror so that I could look at myself. I appreciated this, because it was rare that I actually had the chance to really look at my disabled body. Here, I could inspect my scars—the ones on my belly from my bowel obstruction surgery. I could look down at my purple feet—the ones that don't get enough circulation because I don't walk. I could look at my spastic hands—my left one, I have lovingly referred to as "my claw" since I was about 15. In this daily ritual, I could give myself a real once over, to check how my being crippled fitted me today. Was it too tight? Did it feel out of place, or did it fit just right?

Each and every time we would do this routine together he would look at me in the mirror with a big grin on his face. I remember that he was usually holding my electric razor while doing this, as I usually wanted a shave. Without fail, he would put the razor to my face, smile and say: "We have to make you handsome. We need to find you several wives to marry." The first time he said this to me I wasn't really surprised; there is an assumption that all disabled people are heteronormative, and I knew that he was trying to find some point of connection for the two of us as worker and client. It isn't easy for care attendants to build rapport with clientele; it is a delicate relationship that can take years to build and foster. So, that first time I laughed it off and said something like, "Yup, all the wives." It just made things easier for me, if I went along with it. Who would it hurt if he didn't know I was into guys? The second, third and fourth times this happened, I smiled and played the game. By the 30th or 40th time, I just wasn't answering back when he made the comment to me. I was scared that if I did it would shatter the rapport that I had carefully crafted like a woodsman at work (okay, there *must* be a sex joke about wood in there somewhere).

On about the hundredth time Peter put me in front of that mirror, his sole purpose to make me look presentable for a harem of wives, I had had enough. Without fail, his perfunctory phrase, "We have to make you handsome. We need to find you several wives to marry" passed his lips as it had every other morning for over a year. Instead of staying quiet, instead of playing the game, this time I squeaked out, "Or several husbands" in a quiet, meek whisper. He heard me, and his face completely dropped. That big bright smile I was so accustomed to three times a week was gone in a flash. As I sat there, my crippled body naked, looking at our tableau through the mirror; me in my commode chair with a 6'5" man standing over me, it was daunting. As he looked at me, you could hear a pin drop. Part of me was really worried that this new information, this new piece of me he was being introduced to would scare him away. I was ready for him to walk out and leave me there in my shower chair, unable to complete the care because the act of washing me veered too close for comfort for him. I held my breath as he held my gaze, and then finally said, "Oh, okay, a husband then." I remember exhaling and breathing in a big sigh of relief. He had accepted my identity enough that I could receive care—phew. Funnily enough though, for the rest of that whole 90-minute care booking, I didn't hear him crack a laugh. Not once.

I share this story with you to enter into a chapter on caregiving and queerness. So many of you reading this, who live with disabilities, are queer and who receive caregiving services, probably understand intimately scenarios like the one I described above. You know all too well the discomfort and uneasiness of navigating your queer identity with caregivers who may not have experience with queer identity. You understand why hiding that part of yourself is just easier than revealing it... You'd rather have a shower in peace than defend your right to bring that hot non-binary babe home instead of the girl or guy your care worker may have expected...if they expected you to have sex at all. Been there. You know that sometimes the accessible closet you shove your queerness into during care routines is comfortable now. But, I wonder, how do we come out in care settings? How do we be authentically queer, crippled and cared for? I want to look at some ways that you can do that in this chapter.

I also know there are people reading this who are caregivers to disabled people who identify as queer who may be wondering, "How do I help my consumer feel supported in their sexuality? How do I do this while also respecting and honoring my own boundaries?" You may also be wondering what physical things you may have to do to help your consumer experience sexuality, and I know how daunting that can seem.

Using my own experiences in care as a start, I want to try and provide answers to these questions. The more and more I do this work on sexuality and disability, the more I find I am asked questions about the intersection of caregiving and disabled sexuality, because there never seems to be a clear, concise answer. If I am really honest with you all, there never even seems to be a roadmap to an answer either, and for those of us who need care, and those of us who provide care for others, that is fucking frustrating.

What happens when you ask a care worker for help with a sex toy

When I first started out doing this work in sex and disability, probably about a year or so into establishing myself as a sex educator with disabilities, I was contacted by a sex toy brand asking me to test a product. I said yes almost immediately. I had seen other sex educators do fun and honest reviews, and I was really excited to do one of my own. So, the toy was sent to me. It sat at the post office for weeks. One thing I had forgotten was that I couldn't open boxes on my own, and I would need help with that. Given that I need help with so many daily activities, I'm not too sure how I forgot this vital step, but I did. I was petrified to ask for this kind of help from my caregivers. It had been drilled into my head as a consumer of these caregiving services that there had to be clear and present boundaries, and needing help with opening a sex toy felt like some kind of violation. When you sign up for the kind of attendant care that I receive, the administration sits you down and goes over a huge, bullet-point list of all the things you can and can't do. Mostly it is there to keep the attendant care worker safe and absolve them of any liability should something go wrong, but I can definitely tell you, there is nothing in those forms about helping a client with a sex toy...and there fucking needs to be.

One day, I finally went down to the post office and retrieved the box. I brought it home where, in my trepidation, it sat for another week or so. Every time an attendant walked in, I wanted to ask for help with it, but every time I simply couldn't.

There was one attendant I really, really liked, though. We got along well, and I could talk to her freely about who I was without any hesitation. My queerness and sexuality didn't phase her at all, and I enjoyed her company. One afternoon she was helping me with care, and I blurted out, "I need you to help me try a sex toy." I could feel my face grow hot and flush as the words left my mouth. To my surprise, without hesitation, she said, "Oh, that's no problem. Sure." If you are a caregiver reading this part, her response is how we should all be responding when asked for help with this. Her response opened the door for me to feel safe and supported; it reaffirmed for me that my sexuality didn't have to be hidden away, that it could be addressed openly without fear. I was gobsmacked by her willingness to help me. This had never happened before, and I definitely didn't know how to navigate the next steps, but I was grateful that she had offered.

For a few days after she agreed, she would ask me if I was ready to try and I would decline. Despite her kindness and willingness to facilitate care, I was still pretty unnerved at the idea of the administration finding out that I asked for help with a sex toy. They have rules here that clients aren't even allowed to spend time with the staff outside working hours, so the idea of clients asking for this kind of help felt illegal in some way.

Finally, the night arrived. My attendant (we'll call her Carrie) came into my room at a pre-arranged time. She had a big smile and a little bit of a mischievous twinkle in her eye. "Ready to do this?" she asked, an edge of excitement in her tone. I was, but I was having trouble reconciling my two worlds colliding. My world of care; a place that is sterile, routine, regimented down to the minute, was about to crash into this carefree sexy version of me that I had in my head. That was definitely a mindfuck.

As Carrie was getting all this set in motion, she was putting on gloves and putting down blue pads. I watched her do this, and I felt so disconnected from my sexuality and far too connected to my disability. When I imagined getting off in my head with a toy, I saw candles, soft 90s R&B jams flowing from my iPhone, and an easy, long, intense orgasmic experience. I hadn't factored in the sterile gloves, hospital style blue pads and a second person there. The reality of this was starting to feel thoroughly unsexy, and I'd be lying to you if I said there wasn't a palpable grief that I felt as the fantasy tape in my head stopped with an abrupt, loud click.

Carrie transferred me to my bed and put the toy on my genitals. As she was leaving she said, "Have fun, I'll see you in about 20 minutes." The time limit she had placed on my pleasure was so jarring. I can remember lying there, trying desperately to get into the zone. I had no music that I could play, and I tried screaming at Siri to play "Sexy Jams" to no luck.

I realized as I lay there, prone in my bed with my pants down and this toy wrapped around my balls (quite the image, I know), that I couldn't reach the tiny buttons to change the vibration. I twisted my crippled fingers as best I could, but I accidentally hit a button that made it go way too fast and start to hurt. I could hear the whirring of the machine, and it felt as if my balls were in a vice. I just managed to reach my phone, call the attendant line, and barely squeak out, "Can you send Carrie, please?" Five minutes later, Carrie burst in the room and said, "So, did you bust a nut, friend?" I just rolled my eyes, smiled and asked her to remove the toy from its grip. I'll never forget this experience because it underscored a few things that I think queer disabled people deal with: seeing the medicalization of our bodies crash into the sexualized version of who we wish we could be, but can't really access without help. That stuff is so hard, and no one ever talks about it in disability spaces.

For weeks after this attempt at attendant facilitated pleasure, I felt at odds with my severely crippled body. I withdrew from anything sexual, and I convinced myself that my body was only meant for caregiving help, and that I wasn't allowed anything else. I didn't want time limits on my pleasure, and I certainly didn't want to ask for help that involved blue pads and sterile gloves.

Coming out to care

Eight years ago, when I first moved into my new care home in Toronto, I didn't fully express my queer identity. In fact, for as long as I could I kept it hidden from them. I would use gender neutral pronouns to describe people I was dating or fucking. I tried to keep it as casual as I could. At some point, I couldn't hold it in anymore and I let it slip that I was queer. I remember just saying, "Yeah, I am seeing a guy tonight," to one of the care staff. I thought nothing of it and moved on.

The next thing I knew there were whispers in the attendant

office about my queerness. Apparently, it was the talk of the place for a day or two. One of the attendants told me that everyone's flabbers were ghasted when they knew. This kind of behavior highlights a big problem in care settings: because we don't have a framework to talk about sex and caregiving, anything that deviates even a little bit from cis, white or heterosexual is met with resistance or rumor or ridicule.

Because of all this, I find it particularly difficult to come out about my non-binary identity with care staff. It has become increasingly difficult for me to explain my use of they/he pronouns to caregiving staff who are from other parts of the world, and who may not understand how this all works. Moreover, I don't want to continually unpack what non-binary means with them or explain that I am not a girl or a boy, but a person. In those instances, I feel very privileged that I can hide behind my AMAB (assigned male at birth) identity and shapeshift into more masculine spaces, but my heart also aches for those of us who don't hold that privilege. The shapeshifting I have to do in care spaces definitely takes its toll on who I am and who I want to be.

Carving out space for sexuality, caregiving and disability

I feel we need to carve out moments for caregivers to voice their questions and concerns about caregiving and sex. They need time and resources to unpack their own ableism around sexuality and disability in a space where they aren't shamed for learning about it. What scares them about sex and disability?

What are their socio-cultural understandings of queerness, care and sexuality? How have they unintentionally contributed to ableism in this space? These are key questions that would help caregivers open up the conversation around sexuality within caregiving, and in my experience, those spaces simply don't exist. We throw caregivers and clients together in extremely intimate and personal situationships (yes, I do think wiping my butt can be more intimate than sex) and we don't give either person the tools to navigate that at all. This sends a dangerous message to caregivers that they can't or shouldn't address the sexual health needs of their clients, and ought only to be focused on their bodies and nothing more. Caregivers don't have the opportunity to see their disabled client as a whole person, with queerness and sexuality intact, and that is a big problem.

How can you talk to your caregiving team about queerness?

As a queer disabled person who owns their sexuality, one of the areas that I haven't really mastered is how to talk to your caregiving team about being queer. I think that having these conversations is paramount to a good relationship with your caregiving team—but how? Where do you start? How do you get over the fear? How do you build a rapport that allows your queerness to shine? I don't know if I have all the answers to these questions, but I'd like to at least lay down a foundation, so that should you need to have that chat with a caregiver, you have a resource you can refer to.

Where do you start the conversation?

I think that one of the best ways to start the conversation around care and queerness is to state your queerness right at the beginning. Whether that be during the interview process—naming your queer identity there—or during your first shift with them, the sooner the better. This way you have set the groundwork for who you are. The conversation can be as simple as, "Hi! I'm Andrew. I want to let you know, before we start working together, that I am queer and disabled. If you have any questions about that, please let me know." I know that may seem really formal, but it opens the door to discussion, and it is a little bit softer than saying, "I'm queer and crippled. Deal with it, will you?"

How do you get over your fear of coming out to care?

Starting the conversation around queerness and disability can be really, really scary. The fear of wanting to share that part of yourself, but not knowing how to do so, can impact the way that you interact with your caregiver, and ultimately impact the kind of experience you have with them. It can lead to awkward hour-long silences during care shifts, not dressing in the clothes that you want because you fear being judged (I have a dinosaur dress my mom bought me, one that I have been dying to wear. I haven't though, because I've been far too scared about what my caregivers would think about a guy wearing a dress).

I don't know if you ever get over that fear, but you can

practice working on it. You can write out what you want to say, so that you know exactly the words that describe your queer experiences. Then position your mobility aid in front of the mirror and practice saying, "Caregiver, I want to let you know that I am queer, and here is what that means for our relationship. Here's what I'll need from you to feel confidently crippled and queer when we work together." Put your own spin on it, and see how it feels to take the first shot on your own. Naming the connections between queerness, care and disability out loud to yourself, and then to caregivers, will build, deepen and strengthen the rapport you have with your attendant.

How do you build a rapport that allows both your queerness and your disability to shine?

In 2014, I hosted the world's first disabled sex party in Toronto, Canada (okay, I am sure that it wasn't the world's first). The night of the event, one of my attendants who had never done my care before was the only one available to help me. I remember that I had to ask him to help me put on a leather harness. It was a beautiful piece of clothing, and it accentuated my perky crippled nipples. He struggled to put it on me, and kept muttering how hard it was to do, and questioning why I was even wearing this, and why couldn't I just go *normally*. All of the excitement for the event had been deflated; any joy I had about this upcoming milestone I was going to embark on had left me, and I remember leaving for the event that night ashamed that I needed help with a sexy harness at all.

Building a rapport with a caregiver to talk about queerness

doesn't have to be as intense as asking for help with a sex toy or wearing a dress. One of the lighter ways that I have built rapport with my caregivers is to talk about my celeb crushes. I found that the easiest way to gauge their comfort level with parts of my identity is to use Hollywood as the backdrop. So, sometimes I will talk about my fave celeb who gives me the tingles, and see how they react. If we can laugh about my crush together, I know that I won't have that much more heavy lifting to do when I have to explore other parts of my queerness.

Other ways that you can build a rapport with your attendant care worker around your queer identity or sexuality is to talk about it openly with them on a consistent basis. Perhaps you could bring up your need for help setting up masturbation toys with them every day. Or you could explain to them that you hook up sometimes and you want to be fresh and ready, and will need help with that. A few of my attendants help me prep for sexual encounters by helping me wash and clean beforehand. There is also a big comfort in having someone get me ready for sex, because I can let them know who I am with and ensure my safety.

Funny moments of queerness and care

This rapport building is not always easy or fun for me; it has been fraught with insecurity and uncertainty. But, for all that disability discomfort that I have had to endure owning my queerness in care spaces, there have been great moments. I remember once when I worked with an attendant to calm my gag reflex down because I wanted to get better at giving oral sex. I was frustrated with the reality that because of my cerebral palsy, I would gag on most things, from toothbrushes to medication. The day we practiced, my attendant was helping me breathe and stay calm. When I connected with the comedy of what I was actually doing in the moment, I started to giggle uncontrollably. Without thinking, I quipped, "I hope that I can choke on something that I enjoy." My attendant broke out laughing too, and the boundary that we had between us fell away amid squeals of laughter. That is a moment that I love so much, and can't ever forget.

Crippled coitus interrupted

Remember the hot threesome that I told you about in Chapter 3? Well, it was actually something that I had planned for my 35th birthday. I wanted to do something wild and crazy, and that threesome felt like the perfect escape...and befitting for a birthday gift. Even though I had the internalized ableism to contend with in that moment, what I didn't share with you was that the day of the threesome also happened to be the day that the attendant team picked up my laundry. Every Thursday between 1 and 3pm, two of my attendants would come in to bring me back my laundered clothes. Now knowing my sex date fell on laundry day, I had told three different attendants to help me reschedule it, but when seven people are charged with taking care of 19 people, each with complex disabilities, things can be lost in translation. This happens all the time in caregiving situations.

There I was trying to fellate and pleasure two of the hottest men that I have ever had in my room (or anywhere in my vicinity for that matter) and just as we were getting in the groove, I heard my door unlock and my attendant's sweet voice lilting in above the moans of pleasure below. When my lovers realized that a woman had entered our scene unexpectedly, being able-bodied they jumped up as fast as they could to cover themselves, while I lay there, a crumpled, cripple mess of cum and embarrassment. Looking back on this moment, I laugh, because something like this would only happen to a disabled person who needed care, and I think it is important to highlight these moments for people who don't need care (yet), so they can understand the simultaneously precious and precarious ways in which privacy, when you are severely disabled, isn't a thing you get to engage with fully.

Finding our way through queerness and care is like a maze; one in which there are no instructions, and the pieces keep changing right when you least expect it. No one tells you how to talk to a caregiver about your queer identity, and that sucks. But, it can be done. You can be your whole self with your caregiving team, I promise you. A word of advice from me, though: to do it most effectively, you may want to move laundry day if you are able to.

CHAPTER 7

Learning How to Cultivate Queer Disabled Connection Through Failure, But Ultimately Land on Queer Disabled Joy

I have been in search of a queer crippled connection with my community for years. One of the key things that I have learned while on my quest to make those bonds stick is that despite your best efforts, you will fail at this. Sometimes, those failures will be spectacularly funny, other times they will hurt like fuck. As this chapter is all about finding queer disabled joy, I thought it might be important to share with you some of my biggest attempts at connection that resulted in some pretty big fails.

The white van

I remember one night when I was in my early twenties in my dorm room. It was nearing the end of our spring semester and almost everyone had moved out of student housing. I was staying there over the summer so that I could still receive my daily attendant care. If I'm honest with you, dear reader, on this particular night in question, I was jonesing for some queer cripple connection. To put it more plainly, I wanted to get laid. I remember hopping online and chatting with a few guys who looked like suitable bedmates for the evening. After a few hours of chatting, flirting and bumping up against the mindless ableism that persists in digital spaces ("Oh no, what happened?" "Oh, you are far too much work for me. No thanks."), a cute older couple caught my attention. (I can't help but laugh as I write this, because I am the age now that this couple was then. Wow, how time flies.) I remember that they had been looking for a threesome with a younger guy, and it seemed as though I fitted the bill. Because I was so starved of connection and any kind of intimacy that would allow me freedom to access my queer identity, I didn't hesitate or think twice when they suggested that they would come over in their unmarked white van and take me back to their place. Without considering what I was doing, I agreed.

They came over on a Saturday night around 11pm to pick me up from the dormitory. They were both extremely attractive to me at the time, and I was so enamored at the fact that they would be willing to sleep with me, I am sure I overlooked some glaring red flags in my quest for connectivity. They very quickly realized that they couldn't actually lift my 300lb power wheelchair into their van. I remember them lifting me into the front seat of their van, and waiting patiently while I heard them grunt and struggle to lift it. As I sat there in these strangers' van, it never crossed my mind just how easily what I was doing could have morphed into a *Dateline* exclusive (as a true crime lover, I would absolutely die to have Keith Morrison say my name, but I just don't want to be dead for that to happen).

Finally, I suggested that they bring my collapsible shower chair instead because it was lighter. One of the guys went into my dorm, grabbed the chair and threw it into the van, and off I went with two strange men in search of connection.

When we got to their place and they carried me inside so that we could have small talk before our clothes came off, I remember looking at their walls. I saw loads of photos of a happy couple, two people who genuinely cared about each other; wedding photos, out at bars together, all the kinds of photos two non-disabled queer men can take without a care in the world. I can still remember the pang of want as I looked at those pictures of them. I so wanted that bond, that connection, and I longed that I would never have to fight through all the ableism I do to have it. Some 20 years on, I still have that pang of want; a wish that hopefully, one day, someone will see me, just as I am, my body full of the palsy, and say, "Yup, he's the one."

Back to the story. After I was in their house, both gentlemen were out of breath from trying to carry me inside. I remember one of them who had been tasked by his partner to hold on to my top half whispering, "This is going to be a lot of work." It was at this point, I'm pretty sure, it may have dawned on each of them that due to my disabilities, I wasn't going to be the easy one-nighter they had been in search of. I was going to need caregiving during our casual tryst. To their credit, they powered through helping me to have sex. They took off my clothes, and we went through the motions of a hookup, but they didn't actually engage with me at all. I was just sort of there. I can remember feeling upset in this moment because my search for connection had yet again been a failure, and whether it was true or not, I blamed my disability. If I were able-bodied, these handsome men would have seen me differently, surely. When we were finished they helped me to put my clothes back on, acting as if all of this care was some sort of big favour they were doing me.

They drove me back in their unmarked white van, and while I was out of harm's way physically (seriously, though, how fucking lucky was I that these guys didn't hurt me?), it was painful to reconcile with the truth that perhaps my needs were too much for these two non-disabled guys. I thought to myself as I slunk back to my room, "When will my needs actually be enough for someone? When will they not be afraid to engage with me?" These are thoughts that still rattle around in my head today.

I waited all night

In another attempt at finding queer disabled joy and connection, I remember hooking up with this guy online. From what I remember of him, the picture he had was really cute. Looking back on this, I now realize that he was probably using a stock photo of a "hot guy," but it was 2006 and my internet literacy was not where it is today (to be honest, it's not come on much further...LOL). He told me that he wanted me to come to his place; that he had a big house all to himself (again, looking back at this, the hugest of red flags). I jumped at the chance to do something like this, because so many of my hookups were staid and in my home. This makes sense now due to accessibility, of course. At home, I have all the crippled comforts that I need to be okay. On the flip side to that, though, if a guy comes into my home, they instantly see just how disabled I am. That is something that I can't stand. Because I never really had, or even today have, the chance to go to a guy's place to hook up, it's kind of the ultimate fantasy for me. Think of going through the wardrobe in the Narnia books. That's what going to a guy's place feels like for me.

I was so excited that I hopped in an accessible taxi at 10pm and did as the guy instructed me: waited outside his big house for him to come and get me. It was October and I wasn't dressed properly because I wanted to seem "sexy." Basically, I was freezing. I waited five minutes, then ten minutes more passed, and then an hour. I was so hungry to connect with someone and to be seen as a sexually viable partner regardless of my disability that I stood there and waited three hours for this guy to come get me. He never did. By the time that I called a wheelchair taxi, it was too late and they advised me there weren't any on the road. I had to wait two more hours for an accessible cab to come, and when I finally made it home and logged on to the site to find out why the fuck I was left sitting out there, he told me that he had seen my wheelchair through his window and he had decided that I was too ugly for him, and so he just didn't show.

Even thinking back on that memory is soul-crushing because it reminds me just how much ableism people have around disabled folks—especially young non-disabled queer people. I also remember being so angry that I had failed at this connection because I just wanted a regular sketchy hookup, like every other 20 something queer kid. Instead, I got walloped in the face by ableism, yet again. There is no pretending that didn't sting then, and I can't pretend that it doesn't sting now.

These stories of failure to find queer disabled joy are hard to recount, but I hope that they act as a reminder to you that so many of us go through these things as disabled queer people and that you are not alone in your quest to find queer disabled joy through intimacy.

The staircase

Now I want to share a story that, looking back on it, fills me with queer disabled joy.

There was a guy I met outside a bar once when I was walking home from my friend's rock show one night back in 2007. He was older than me but we took a liking to one another almost immediately. We ended up making out that night outside the bar like two teenagers in heat. It was pretty hot. I remember telling a friend about what happened with him, giddily excited to share my exploits. When I told her about him and showed her a grainy photo on my Nokia phone, she steered me away from him. Wanting to be cool, every time I went out with this friend, I deliberately avoided his advances.

After our makeout session, he left me his number, and one night when I was all alone and a bit lonely about my lack of a sex life, I called him. I told him that I wanted to hook up with him and spend some time together. I'll never forget what happened next: within 20 minutes there was an accessible cab at my door taking me to his apartment. When I got there, he came to get me but we realized that he had no elevator to his unit. Without thinking about it, he casually said, "I'll carry you up the stairs." I was so excited by the prospect of a man carrying me anywhere that I said "Yes!" In the dead of winter, he parked my power chair at the corner of his building in between a little hole so that no one would steal it. (Do not do this. This is 100 percent how wheelchairs and other mobility aids get stolen. No matter how hot the person is, I repeat, *do not do this.*)

I remember that he scooped me up in his arms and started walking the six or seven flights up the fire escape to his apartment window. I felt as if I was in an episode of every teen drama at the time as we went through his window. While he was out of breath from carrying me, it didn't deter him one bit from seeing me as sexually viable. We made out and had great sex, never once bumping up against my disability as a barrier. At the time that felt revolutionary, and almost 20 years on it still feels the same way.

At one point during our sexcapade, I had to pee. I was terrified because I knew that I needed his help to do this, and I knew that it was probably the most unsexy thing to ask someone in the middle of intimacy. Then, the coolest thing happened. He jumped up, glowing from our sex, and asked, "What do you need me to do?" He ran to his kitchen and grabbed a Coke bottle from the fridge, emptied its contents in his sink, cut a hole in it and said, "Will this do?" with a huge motherfucking grin on his face that I still remember now. I like this tale as it is a reminder that even though access to sexuality as disabled queer people can be fraught with misunderstandings, danger and ableism, there are still people who are willing to take a chance to help you experience queer disabled joy.

Here's another queer crippled memory that helped me understand there is queer disabled joy in connection, even if it doesn't always work out.

The eight pack

I had just moved from my college town to my very first post-college town apartment in a small hamlet an hour north of Toronto, called Richmond Hill. I was lonely because I had left all my college friends in that town where I had lived for the past nine years. While I felt alone, I also felt that it was a chance to start anew, to see who was out there. Okay, okay, who am I kidding here? I was excited to see the kind of guys I could meet in a new city. By this time in 2013, hookup apps had become way more prevalent in the queer community, so I was on them fairly consistently, hunting for anti-ableist lovers. Once I got settled into my new place I was ready to christen it with someone new. Because I require caregiving to get into bed at night I usually had a firm bedtime of 11pm, but one night I managed to arrange to stay up a few hours later.

During that time, I went on the apps and met "Eight pack." He lived in Toronto, but he thought I was cute and took the subway and then a taxi all the way to my apartment. I kid you not, friends, when he stepped out of the cab, it looked as if an Abercrombie and Fitch model had just emerged. I was hooked. He grabbed my face and told me how handsome I was, and kissed me without hesitation—a thing that to this day hasn't happened since. He was insatiable for me and my disabled body, lifting me out of my wheelchair with ease and no fear whatsoever. As he peeled off the shirt that tightly clung to him, I counted that he had an eight pack instead of a six-pack. It was a new experience for me, having someone who embodied able-bodied privilege to its core, find someone like me (the exact polar opposite of that) attractive. It was thrilling and we had sex all night long.

I remember waking up next to him absolutely petrified because I knew that my caregiving team would be coming to wake me up, and I wasn't ready for someone this hot to see just how much care I needed. Once he saw that he would definitely run off. I was sure of it. He rolled awake next to me, kissed me and said, "Oh, did you want to shower with me and go for breakfast?" I hesitated, knowing that this meant he would see my care routine, but as he lay there next to me, his big brown eyes beaming, I couldn't resist. I said, "Fuck yes!" canceled my caregiver for the morning, and let him help me with the routine. I remember that he took so much care to ensure that he was doing it the way I needed him to, while simultaneously making it really sexy and sensual. It showed me for one of the first times in my adult life that there is joy in caring for someone. We had sex in my shower and I felt really connected to him. Afterwards, he put me in my wheelchair and we went for breakfast at the diner across the street. He held my hand as we walked there, and I remember feeling whole. Throughout our whole breakfast I yammered on about the next time we'd see each other, and he seemed interested in pursuing something.

After our whirlwind date, I called him a few times to reconnect but we never did. I never saw him again. I was angry at first, worried that someone like that wouldn't come around again, but now with hindsight, I understand that there is a joy in knowing that I had the experience at all, that someone saw me in all my crippled realness—my twisted toes, curved spine and all the weight that held—and chose to stay.

Things that bring me queer disabled joy! (And how you can cultivate queer disabled joy for yourself too)

Let me tell you some stories of the things that help my queer crippled heart hum and then leave you with some notes to find ways to find your own joy amid all the ableism. It isn't fucking easy, but you can do it. Let's crack on in.

Sharing my truth as a severely disabled person brings me queer crippled joy

It may seem funny considering this whole book (and my whole professional persona) is anchored by my disability, but I find talking about my disability really difficult. I always worry that I am saying the wrong things about disability, or that I am not doing disability activism right at all. I worry that because I identify as a severely disabled person who needs ongoing care, my story is often sidelined for the more inspirational ones— the ones pedaled by media outlets that help us feel good about ourselves, and during many times in my life that's been the truth. People don't want to hear that I need help in the washroom or that I couldn't shower for 12 days in 2021 because of a caregiving shortage brought on by the pandemic. They want to hear that I stood up and walked thanks to an exoskeleton, or that I have beaten the odds and done something miraculous. The truth is, as a severely disabled person I haven't done any of those big budget things, and I won't ever do them. But, what I can do is to share my truth as a severely disabled person using platforms on social media to highlight those realities.

Just the other day, I was feeling down and self-pitying and I needed a dopamine hit. I asked my followers to tell me what they liked about my work. I got a flood of messages telling me that my honesty around disability is refreshing, and that some people who interact with my posts feel less alone by seeing me there, telling my raw, disabled truth. That's powerful, knowing that my words about disability, about experiences that scare the shit out of me, have impacted people to learn, to feel connected and to engage with disability. Knowing that I have been able to add my voice to the next generation of disability learning is something that humbles me but also makes me so proud.

WHAT YOU CAN DO

I encourage anyone reading this right now, especially if you are disabled, to start sharing your experience of disability. Write it in a post, make a voice note, start a podcast, write a letter to yourself, whatever it looks like for you—share it. It isn't meant to be easy, hell, it isn't fun sometimes, but it will have a ripple effect for years to come that will shape disability policy, queer rights and so much more. Disabled voices need your queer crippled realness. Do it!

If you are reading this and you aren't disabled, I encourage you to listen to the disabled queer people around you. Reflect on what you might want when you yourself encounter disability. How will you want to be treated? Think about the ways in which you have contributed to ableism. I'd recommend you be gentle with yourself here—it is everywhere we look—and strive to do better when and how you can. It will be you one day, and you can secure your disabled joy for tomorrow.

Being the only queer cripple in the room brings me queer disabled joy (and is powerful as fuck)

I remember in 2015 I was asked to be part of a video and photo series about queer masculinity. I told the organizers that they needed disabled people in the room like me, and so I was accepted. One of the first things we were asked to do was take our clothes off in the group. As I wheeled my power chair into the room, I saw that I was the only wheelchair user out of all these men. Right then and there I could have left, feeling different and unrepresented among them all, and believe me, I wanted to. Their bodies didn't look like mine in any way. As I watched everyone around me undress, I realized that I needed help. Two of the guys jumped in to help me, and we took the photos. I am still so proud of doing that, and for being the only wheelchair user in the room. It sends such a message, and every time I'm the only one in a sea full of queer bodies, I remember how much power I actually have. That brings me fucking joy.

WHAT YOU CAN DO

If you are disabled and queer and are the only one at a party, an event or in the room wherever that may be, remember that you are powerful in this moment. You hold all the crip cards here. Enjoy the fuck out of it. It's so important—I promise. You are sending a message to people that you deserve to be in this space, while simultaneously signaling to the world who isn't here that should be. This is especially important for those with invisible or dynamic disabilities. If you are the only one in that room, speak about it—the louder you are, the sooner you won't be the only one.

If you are not disabled and you're reading this part thinking,

"How do I make sure there is more than one disabled person at my event?" I have the answer for you. Ready? Hire disabled people and pay them to consult for you. They can guide you in more ways than you realize, not only to recognize what inclusion looks like, but what it *feels* like too. That's an important and often overlooked distinction that needs to be better understood.

Talking disabled sex brings me queer crippled joy

I am so thankful for the funny, awkward, weird, good, bad, strange experiences that I have had when it comes to my sexuality. I still don't think I've had the best sex of my disabled life, and who knows if I will, but the fact that I have had these experiences in the bedroom is important because it shows me that we are all learning. I love that I can be someone's first disabled lover, and I love that I can share my that in presentations so that people can confront their own ableism around it.

I remember doing a presentation once showing stills from my first adult film I was a part of, talking to the audience about the importance of representation and visualization of these things, and how so many people were thankful because they'd never seen anything like that before. Being the person in the room who can help alter someone's worldview around sexuality and disability is something that I beam about, and I can't tell you the full extent of joy that brings me.

WHAT YOU CAN DO

If you are queer and disabled, and if you feel safe and comfortable to do so, talk about your sex life where you can. Sexuality and disability are pathologized and discounted by so many and you have an opportunity to make waves there. I know how hard it can be to even think about sex when you're disabled and you have so much else to contend with just to have your day go okay. Maybe you start by talking about sex and disability to yourself. What about it brings you joy? Then keep the conversation going and see what happens.

Notes from a queer cripple to you: Thanks for reading

When I started this project, I didn't know what I wanted it to be. Over the course of writing these "notes," I have learned so much about myself, my queerness and my disability. These stories were not easy to discuss, but I felt they were necessary for you to hear and for me to tell. I hope that they have made you laugh, cry, squirm, howl, think, reflect and consider all the ways in which disability is a part of queerness, and vice versa. If you are a queer disabled reader, I hope you saw yourself in this somewhere. If you picked this up and you aren't disabled, I hope you learned a lot, and you have questions about what you can do next. I am so proud to be a queer cripple and to share these notes with you, friends! Xo, Andrew!